Depressive Illness
and the Christian

Elaine Wright

LIGHTHOUSE
PUBLISHING

© Elaine Wright 2019

Published by: Lighthouse Publishing
Grieves Cottage, Drumelzier Haugh Farm
Broughton
Biggar
ML12 6JD

British Library Cataloguing in Publication Data.
A catalogue record for this book is available

ISBN: 978-1-9108483-3-3

Cover design: Esther Kotecha, EKDesigns
Layout by: Angela Selfe

Printed in the United Kingdom

For
Chris and Kate
who, in themselves,
gave me the best reasons
to keep putting one foot in front of the other

Acknowledgements

I would like to thank, first of all, my friend Sue, who led me to Christ, helped me so much in the early days and continues to be a faithful friend. To my husband Richard, thank you for your love, patience and support, especially in my darker days and in the writing of this book. I would also like to thank Rev. John Ross for encouraging me in the writing of a course for Christians with a depressive illness and allowing me to run it at Farnham Baptist Church.

Finally, I would like to thank my faithful team of co-workers and valued friends who have been working on courses with me over the years, and who, despite having their own struggles with depression, have been willing to give up their time, share their stories and offer so much help and encouragement to others: Irene Parry, Alison Edwards, Richard Feltham, Wendy Soane and Helen Tilley.

Contents

Foreword

It was the autumn of 2017 when I met the author of this gem of a book, Elaine Wright. Immediately I felt that I had met someone who really understood what it felt like to struggle with depression: not only how difficult it is to suffer with this awful illness, but often the added perceived or literal stigma if you are a sufferer of the illness and a Christian.

The first diagnosis I had of depression was before I became a Christian. It was after the birth of my second, much wanted daughter, when post-natal depression took hold. (I suspect I had suffered with depression from my teen years without realising it.) However, back then the stigma was immense and I told only the people closest to me in case people thought I was a failure as a mother. Things have changed radically over recent years, where those outside the church seem to be often more sympathetic than those who profess to follow Jesus.

When I became a Christian, I felt a whole lifetime of depression lift off me and that continued until I was a curate – sixteen years later. For several different reasons, the depression returned, and while I should have felt able to share my struggles and not feel shame or embarrassment, this was not the case. To be a Christian and depressed was hard enough, but to be a church leader seemed to bring a whole new level of shame. It was during this time I did the 'Depressive Illness and the Christian' course with Elaine and her team. The sense of relief that came about through this wonderful course was quite profound. To hear that I wasn't weak and a failure, but the complete opposite, brought a whole new sense of worth, as well as a feeling that God could in fact use this time for His purposes too.

As a church leader I would say that depression is the illness that I encounter most often. I believe there is an epidemic of mental health issues and there are many factors contributing to it. It's easy to want to simplify it, but this disease is complex and affects people whose lives appear stable to the outside world. As Elaine points out, "We won't know when meeting a person with a depressive illness what has gone before."

As the Church we need to get much better at caring for those with mental illnesses. I believe this book and the course that it is derived from are tools that we can use to bring the care necessary to our congregations and the wider church body.

The book gives examples of Bible characters who possibly may have been struggling with depression – showing that God uses all those who surrender to Him regardless of whether they have everything sorted. It also has practical advice if you are struggling yourself or caring for someone with the illness, as well as prayers to help the person suffering with issues associated with this illness.

I for one am glad that Elaine has written this very accessible and readable book and it is my hope and prayer that as you read it, if you are suffering with depression, you will feel the Lord walking through the pages with you and speaking to you about how to begin the slow recovery from this awful illness.

Rev. Antonia Elliott
Community Minister
Arborfield Green

In Others' Words

This book will be a really useful aid for those who cannot attend the course itself as well as those who can. It contains the key concepts that helped me to move, over time, from a state of hopelessness back to a place where I could interact with life at home and work. My thanks to Elaine and those who helped me.

Pavinder Mehet
Holy Trinity Church, Aldershot, Hants

I have found "Depressive Illness and the Christian" extremely helpful in understanding that God is with me and not against me in my struggle with depression. I found the section on spiritual armour particularly helpful – it helped me to understand more about the tactics the enemy uses to try and defeat us and the protection that we have to defend ourselves. I have had the privilege of working with Elaine on the course for a few years now and there is always something new that the Lord teaches me. I think the book will be extremely helpful to other Christians suffering with depression. It has been created by someone who has suffered with depression herself and found help from God through His Word.

Alison Edwards, Depressive Illness and the Christian team and
Support Group Leader
Farnham Baptist Church

I originally discovered the 'Depressive Illness and the Christian' course when I was suffering with suspected depression. As a Christian I found that this course gave me greater insight into the Biblical perspective of the illness, which alongside the medical treatment gave me tools to help me recover.

As depression is a lonely illness, with sufferers not talking about it and non-sufferers not understanding it, the course, and this book, explains the illness by highlighting Biblical characters who suffered, and God's care and help for them. It shows you are not alone in your feelings, and even when you feel totally alone, God is there by your side.

It is my hope that this book will help non-sufferers to understand the illness better and those who suffer to be encouraged that there is hope for the future.

Richard Feltham, Depressive Illness and the Christian team
St Saviour's, Guildford

This book gives a holistic view of depressive illness combined with medical support. Elaine explores and explains the Biblical view of being a Christian with anxiety and depression. I have been involved with the 'Depressive Illness and the Christian' course from the beginning. This book expands on the Biblical truths which are there for our help, support and guidance.

Irene E Parry, Depressive Illness and the Christian team and
Support Group leader
Farnham Baptist Church

Preface

Depressive Illness is a horrible condition for anyone to deal with. Symptoms include feelings of; disconnection, vulnerability, anxiety, failure, overwhelming tiredness and a deep sense of hopelessness. But for the Christian, there is the added sense of separation from God, leading to feelings of; guilt (because I must have done something wrong), shame (because I should be doing better), fear of judgement (from others who probably think the same) and often the question, "Am I really a Christian after all?" Depression undermines Christian faith in ways that are often difficult for non-sufferers to understand.

I too was diagnosed with post-natal depression nearly twenty-nine years ago. Looking back, I realise I was struggling long before I had children. I took the prescribed medication to help me over what I considered, at the time, to be a 'hurdle', and began to feel better – better than I had done for many years. Unfortunately, that 'hurdle' has taken longer than anticipated to overcome as depressive illness has crept up on me over the years; but, on a positive level, it has helped shape the faith I have today.

With God's help, I have learned to walk with Him through many dark times and grow in my understanding of His acceptance of me, as I am. I have learned to deal with 'what is' rather than what I think (or others think) my life should be. If there have been changes to be made, they have happened gradually, and as I come out of the 'dark tunnels', I am often aware that God has woven something new into my character. This is what scripture tells us will happen: ". . . we know that suffering produces perseverance, perseverance character; and character, hope" (Romans 5:3-4).

I am grateful for the definite times when God has led me to see my GP when I haven't been coping – patiently waiting for me to put my resistance and reluctance to one side. I have been grateful too for the prescribed medication and kindness from my doctor. Rather than getting in the way of my walk with God, anti-depressants have helped me to maintain my Christian walk and continue to do the things He is calling me to do. On the contrary, without the medication, my abilities to relate to others and God are impaired as I withdraw into myself, which is one of the effects of depression.

As for the cause of the illness, I am content to leave that with God. Like many others, for me, there has been more than one component. Post-natal depression has physiological roots rather than psychological ones, so medication has been a welcome help and solution. However, there have also been some spiritual and emotional roots which God has been dealing with too. I believe myself to be in a 'win-win' situation with God. Either I am learning through difficulty or I am being the grateful recipient of His healing grace bringing me to new places of release and freedom.

God, I have discovered, is a lot kinder to me than I have previously been on myself. He seems to be saying, "This is where you are and this is the help you need." If God is giving me permission to work through this illness as I am, I know this is what He wants for others too. I hope that the following pages will provide help and encouragement especially for those Christians trapped by feelings of guilt, failure, discouragement and despair.

Elaine Wright
September 2019

CHAPTER ONE

Depressive Illness – an epidemic

In a recent news release, the World Health Organisation states, "Depression is the leading cause of ill health and disability worldwide . . . more than 300 million people are now living with depression, an increase of more than 18% between 2005 and 2015."[1] In 2003, Dr Tim Cantopher, from the Priory Clinic in Woking, wrote, "Life, sadly, is getting more stressful and as it does so an epidemic of depressive illness is underway – up to 1 in 3 consultations in general practice involve patients with the disease."[2] Writing for The Independent in 2016, Geraldine Bedell reports that "rates of depression and anxiety among teenagers have increased by 70 percent in the past 25 years"[3]. To sum up, *depression is affecting people all over the world, it is spoken of as an epidemic and the fastest growth rate is seen among the young.* And Christians are not immune.

About thirteen years ago I began to develop a growing desire to help other Christians with depression. I knew that I was not the only one in our church to have this kind of struggle and I knew how God had been helping me. But I found that people were not really open to talking about their depression, and those that did seemed to find their Christian life and walk were 'on hold' whilst they struggled to find the help they needed, usually outside the church. I discovered that many feared the judgement of other

Christians and were finding it hard to pray and ask for God's help. They also carried a real sense of guilt, shame and personal failure.

In 2006, at Farnham Baptist Church, we ran some evening seminars and *Depression* was one of the topics. A Christian psychiatrist, Dr Ruth Fowke, came to speak on the subject to a large audience of Christians looking for insight and answers. The focus of the talk was depression itself, but in the feedback received afterwards, we learned that people would have liked more links to the Bible. I began to pray and ask God about this and whether my own experience of depression and testimony could be helpful in some way. As a consequence, in 2007, I wrote a short Bible-based course called 'Depressive Illness and The Christian' specifically to address the problems being faced by Christians. It seemed to me very obvious that Christians with a depressive illness had an additional set of problems to overcome that the non-believing sufferer would never encounter.

First of all is the very negative way the illness makes them feel about themselves as Christians and their status before God. Since depression puts Christians in a complete spiritual wilderness, it is easy for them to conclude that God has somehow abandoned them. Some might interpret this sense of abandonment as confirmation of poor performance in their walk and witness and a need to try harder. Some may even feel that depression is God's judgement against them, leading to additional feelings of guilt, shame, discouragement and despair. Many will certainly conclude that God is not interested in them when they are ill like this. The struggle is often centred around the question, "How can I, as a Christian, be depressed?" Depressive illness for Christians carries with it a particularly difficult internalised stigma to contend with.

Second is the direct consequence of the *external stigma* many have encountered within their church. Over the years, on our courses, we have heard accounts from Christians from different churches who have felt hurt and undermined by the words and actions of others. Some have felt pushed to the margins because they could no longer participate in the mission focus of their church, and some have been led to question whether they are really Christians at all. When those in the church have perceived their struggle as a sign of weakness needing to be addressed through extra prayer, examination of a sinful past (or present), *or* more Bible reading, their problems have been further compounded. As a consequence, many have found their faith beginning to struggle. When this happens, where do they go from there? Who do they talk to then? Probably not anyone in their church and probably not to God either.

No-one *means* to cause problems by what they say and do. However, it is the case that many Christians with a depressive illness have found that instead of their church being the safest place to be, it has at times been the hardest. For these reasons, everyone who works on the Depressive Illness and The Christian course with me are Christians with their own experience of depression. Empathy has been a necessary qualification in this ministry to reach those Christians who are struggling just to keep going, *and* who have been damaged and hurt by the words and actions of others in their own church family. Attitudes are beginning to change, but it may take some considerable time before the notions and assumptions that sit behind the stigma are properly laid to rest in the minds of those struggling, *and* where they still exist in some areas of the church.

Another challenge being faced by Christians with a depressive illness is where to go to get the *right kind* of help. Some Christians, finding that their churches are ill-equipped to deal with matters of this nature, rely heavily on the work and theories being developed in the secular world, which at the time of writing, has much to say in the area of 'wellness' and 'well-being'. Whilst some may offer a degree of help, we need to be aware that secular theories and philosophies, by definition, will always *"depend on human tradition and the basic principles of this world rather than on Christ"* (Colossians 2:8) and the scripture warns against the possibility of being taken "captive" by them (v8).

The Depressive Illness and the Christian course was written and developed to point Christians back to God in their time of need; to find encouragement in scripture and guidance through prayer. In my own experience of searching for answers, I was struck by these words from Isaiah 45:22, *"Turn to me and be saved."*

In the following chapters I will share some of the things learned over the last twelve years of running courses and praying with others. The chapters themselves are in the order in which we introduce and discuss the topics through presentations and group discussions. I will also share some of the insights gained over the last thirty years, through my own personal struggle with depression, and how God has used it to develop my faith and trust in Him. What I hope to show is that God is *for* people with this kind of struggle and not *against* them (as many of the arguments behind the stigma would seem to suggest). I also hope to show that the Bible has a great many insights, promises and answers for Christians struggling with depression.

The scriptures I have used are ones that God has led me to in my own personal times of depression, and others He has led me to as the course has developed over the years. Unless stated otherwise, I have used the 1984 New International Version translation. I have referenced writings by other Christians whose insights have been extremely helpful and who themselves stay close to scripture. I also make a number of references to Dr Tim Cantopher's paper, *Depressive Illness the Curse of the Strong*, written during his time at the Priory Clinic in Woking. I have found his work invaluable in countering the completely wrong notions that exist in people's minds about both the sufferer and the illness itself.

I also hope to show how scripture is not in agreement with the question, "How can a Christian be depressed?," suggesting that we can be one or the other, but not both. We only have to look at Job and Elijah as examples of godly men whose circumstances led them to want to give up on life altogether to know that we *can* be both, and sometimes will be. Citing Job and Elijah is also extremely important because many more men come on our courses now than they did initially. Depression is not an illness affecting only women and it is no respecter of age. Over the years we have been pleased to help all age groups, the youngest being nineteen and the oldest eighty-three. I hope the following pages will bring clarity to those who would like to know and understand more.

For those seeking help and encouragement, I have tried to keep the chapters short and manageable, as I know only too well what an effort it can be to open a book of any kind when strength has gone. For those who do open it, I hope and pray that you will change your mind about how God sees you and how you see yourself. I hope too that you will be led and inspired to commit yourself even more deeply to Him who knows how to *"work all things for the good of those who love him"* (Romans 8:28), even depression.

CHAPTER TWO

What is a depressive illness?

Dr Tim Cantopher, Consultant Psychiatrist at the Priory Clinic in Woking, wrote:

"Depressive illness happens when one part of the brain called the limbic system malfunctions . . . when this happens, the part of the system that fails is the transmitter chemicals, serotonin and noradrenaline."[4] According to Dr Cantopher, however it came about, it is important to grasp that a depressive illness is a *physical* illness, not a *mental* one. He writes that, ". . . clinical depression is not a psychological condition or a state of mind. It is a physical illness."[5] This in itself can lift the burden of failure and guilt from a Christian. One of our team has spoken of her relief in discovering that what she had was a 'physical' illness, not a 'mental' one. Since physical illnesses do not carry with them the same stigma as mental illnesses, it took away from her a burden of shame that she had been carrying about herself.

Depression is a physical illness with some potentially very serious symptoms and outcomes. The Christian writer and counsellor Selwyn Hughes wrote that the symptoms can be best described as "feeling[s] of utter hopelessness; despondency, self-disgust, loss of perspective, overall gloom, sadness, apathy, dejection and despair."[6] I have met and prayed with a number of Christians who have had thoughts of suicide, such is the desperate place that this illness can take them. Some have even tried to take their own lives.

If we are to help others on the road to recovery, we must understand the distinction between the *symptoms* and the underlying *physical* cause. If we are telling Christians to try harder, get a grip, pull themselves together, do this or that more, we will not be helping them to get better. As Dr Cantopher writes, ". . . you would not try to overcome pneumonia through exercise or resourcefulness. Neither can you with clinical depression."[7]

The kindest thing we can do for a Christian brother or sister struggling with these kinds of symptoms is to encourage them to go and see their GP, where they can be correctly assessed, diagnosed and treated *as for any other illness.* Even prayer ministry may need to wait until the person is in a more stable place. Medication treats the illness by replacing the lost chemicals in the brain, just as insulin injections provide what is missing in the pancreas of the diabetic. It gives the person time to rest from the disabling symptoms they have been experiencing. And that is what is needed: *rest.* Dr Cantopher writes that in the early stages of recovery this means "avoiding any unnecessary challenges and only, where possible, doing what is easy."[8] In churches this may mean stepping back for a while from things normally undertaken. We must take care not to convey a sense of inconvenience, disappointment or disapproval when a person needs to do this. They will need much love, care and support from their fellowship at such a time. I have met with Christians who feel a great sense of guilt that they are not serving when others are doing so much. We need to be mindful of this and encourage them to know that their health and well-being has to be the priority. Most people with depression are the opposite of lazy and have to learn the valuable lesson of taking time out when they need to.

However, such is the guilt and shame carried by so many Christians, it may take some considerable time before they will even consider going to the doctor. I have found this time and time again. Because I know that it was God who prompted me to take that step, I will always do what I can to persuade them to go and discuss their symptoms with their doctor. At least then they will know whether or not they have a depressive illness and what treatment options are available. Ultimately, though, the decision on whether or not to go is theirs to make.

But one thing we do need to do is show a Christian why they need not feel guilty. The fact is that clinical depression is an *illness,* not a weakness. Furthermore, as we will discover in the next chapter, the typical profile of a person most likely to become ill in this way is one of strength, reliability and diligence, and has nothing at all to do with weakness of character.

CHAPTER THREE

Why a Christian need not feel guilty

One of the things that is most helpful to Christians with a depressive illness is to show them that they are not the weak or failing individuals they have previously thought themselves to be. In fact, they are usually quite the opposite. Dr Cantopher, commenting on stress induced depressive illness, has observed that:

> . . . this illness nearly always happens to one type of person. He or she is strong, reliable, diligent, with a strong conscience and sense of responsibility . . . This is the person to whom you would turn in times of need and [s]he would never let you down. When the going gets tough, this person gets going.[9]

In my view, this profile aptly describes most people with depressive illness, whatever the root cause. The effort and strength needed to get through each day, meeting its demands and challenges, requires a great deal more strength than a healthy person would need to exert and apply. In addition, I have found that same "strong conscience and sense of responsibility" in many people I have spoken to, and it is very often the stress of not living up to their own high expectations of themselves that eventually leads them into depression.

I was first given Dr Cantopher's leaflet by my doctor. He asked me to read it to see if it was helpful. As I read this profile I found myself feeling quite tearful. I had not thought that I had been particularly affected by the stigma attached to depression, but reading it changed my mind. I remember thinking how positive Dr Cantopher's words were, and how kind and encouraging his explanation was of what was really going on. It helped me shed some of the negativity I realised I was holding about myself. I had an illness and the reason had more to do with *strength* than weakness. As a consequence, we give a copy of Dr Cantopher's leaflet to everyone who comes on our courses and point them also to his book of the same name.

Dr Cantopher's words are helpful for Christians and non-Christians alike. But for the Christian, there is often added guilt from the negative reactions of others, especially when it comes from Christian friends or those in their church. The Christian psychiatrist Dr Ruth Fowke wrote, "To state that no follower of Jesus Christ should ever experience disabling nervous distress is a sweeping generalisation [which] is both cruel and dangerous."[10] But that is exactly what *is* being stated by some when they raise the question, "How can a Christian be depressed?" Implicit in that question is the notion that I can be one or the other but not both. For myself, I have to let that be the problem of those asking rather than try to explain it to them. Even after Dr Fowke's seminars on depression at our church, I overheard someone say, "I still don't understand how a Christian can be depressed."

The difficulty for the Christian who hears this in the midst of depression is that on top of everything else their salvation is being called into question at a time when they already feel that God is a long way away. As Dr Fowke has said, it is "both cruel and dangerous". But, as the Bible testifies, in the example of Job, it is also completely wrong. Job's story was of a life overwhelmed by loss, leading him to a place of utter darkness and deep distress, which today we would call depression. But he *was* a godly man. Even God said so: "There is no-one on earth like him; he is blameless and upright, a man who fears God and shuns evil" (Job 1:8). This description of Job, stated twice in Scripture, shows that 'disabling nervous distress' *can* happen to the most faithful of God's servants.

The question "How can a Christian be depressed?" is, therefore, found to be false in its premise, revealing more about the one asking than the one suffering. It is Job's friends who are found guilty by God at the end of the book, not Job.

In the next chapter, as we expose the friends' arguments against Job, we will find a similarity between what they were saying to him and what some have said about Christians with depression in the church, both in its recent history and currently, where the stigma is still a stumbling block. We may conclude that if God was not pleased with the friends, He would not be pleased with those who replicate these arguments in the church either.

CHAPTER FOUR

Job and Job's friends

In the book of Job we meet someone whose life has been traumatised by loss and who has been further afflicted with painful sores, leading him to say, *"I have no peace, no quietness; I have no rest, but only turmoil"* (Job 3:26). The turmoil being described by Job is something many with depressive illness will understand only too well. Job's losses were extreme and severe. Unlike Job's friends, when meeting a person with a depressive illness, we may not know what has gone before. The blows of life for them too may have been severe and many. One of our team has shared that a Christian friend led her to Christ, but when she confided in her that she was depressed, her friend questioned whether her commitment had been 'real'.

Depression is an illness that creeps in over time and usually it will not be down to just one thing. This also negates another question sometimes asked: "What have you got to be depressed about?" as if a person can answer it in a single-sentenced short summary. You might as well say to someone with heart problems, "What have you got to have a heart attack about?" The problems can be so deep-rooted and difficult to locate that a person feels diminished by even trying to answer. And some will not know. Another member of our team said it was others who suggested he might be depressed and advised him to see the doctor. It was only when he discussed with the doctor the breakdown of his marriage and loss of both parents within a short space of time that he began to see where his problems had started and why he was struggling as he was.

But much damage can be done by those who do not have the whole picture on which to base their assumptions, as we see by examining some of the arguments put forward to Job by his friends Zophar, Bildad and Eliphaz.

Firstly, they conclude that Job must have some unconfessed sin in his life which is at the root of his problems. Job does not understand why God would allow his suffering, but he does not believe it is because he has done anything wrong. But his friends are not so sure. Zophar says, "... *if you will put away the sin that is in your hand and allow no evil to dwell in your tent, then you will lift up your face without shame*" (Job 11:14-17).

Assumptions lead people to make judgements which can be damaging and hurtful to a person already in a place of vulnerability. In her book *Through the Dark Woods*, Jo Swinney writes of going to church "feeling as vulnerable as a peeled, hard-boiled egg, deep in depression and misery". She describes wanting to leave as quickly as possible when the service finished but being "collared by a well-meaning, very kind old lady", who "whipped me back in a pew and had me trawling through my wrong-doings, thoughts, words and deeds, so I could repent and thus feel all better. Needless to say, I did not feel better, but rather significantly worse."[11]

Another common question is whether or not the sufferer is doing enough to make themselves better. Bildad says to Job, *"But if you will look to God and plead with the Almighty, if you are pure and upright, even now he will rouse himself on your behalf"* (Job 8:6). Many will use this type of thinking when trying to help Christians with depression, asking "Are you reading your Bible?" or "Are you praying?" as if there is some positive action that has been lacking which could be the key to getting better.

Most people with depression will find it difficult to read the Bible and pray. I was like that. I found that worship music was the best way to feel close to God at times like these. I also learned that God was not waiting for me to get better before He would be active in my life once again. In fact, in my own places of darkness and struggle I have found God in ways which I would not otherwise have done, and my faith has been strengthened by a deepened understanding of His unconditional love for me. I have also found that His help for me usually has nothing to do with what others think I need. In fact, such are the lessons learned that I do not very often share my experiences unless I am with people who understand it for themselves. I really do not want to be on the receiving end of misguided words or advice, however well meant.

Job's friend Eliphaz is sure Job's suffering is God's way of disciplining him. *"Blessed is the man whom God corrects; so do not despise the discipline of the Almighty"* (Job 5:17). But Job's suffering is not anything to do with correction *or* the need for discipline. There is something happening in the unseen realm that the friends do not know about and they base their conclusions on their own limited understanding *and* limited theology. The problem, in that sense, is with the friends rather than with Job – as it is with some in the church. The person who says "I do not understand how a Christian can be depressed" has a similar problem to Job's friends. It sits outside of their theological understanding, leading them to make assumptions which are quite wrong about the person *and* God.

At the end of the book of Job we see God passing judgement against Job's friends. To Eliphaz he says, *"I am angry with you and your two friends, because you have not spoken of me what is right, as my servant Job has"* (Job 42:7). In all the discourses about Job's situation and God's righteousness, judgement and justice, they have not been right about Job or in their witness about God. And in the end God exposes that it is their lack of understanding about Him that leads them to speak out the way they do, and He is angry with them for it.

Many Christians with depression will know only too well Job's anguish of not being able to find God in their situation. *"If I go to the east he is not there; if I go to the west, I do not see him"* (Job 23:8). In that situation people need a lot of reassurance that God has not left them, even though that is how they feel. Those who seem most able to provide this reassurance are Christians who have experienced a depressive illness for themselves. All who work on our courses know what depression is and what it feels like to have it. As a consequence, we do not offer a quick fix; in fact, we do not offer any kind of fix. What we aim to do is *"demolish arguments and every pretension that sets itself up against the knowledge of God . . ."* (2 Corinthians 10:5) and point people back to Jesus, whose arms have been outstretched to them even when they did not know it.

Job was a man of faith and able to say, *". . . but he knows the way that I take; when he has tested me, I shall come forth as gold"* (Job 23:10). Learning to *"live by faith, not by sight"* (2 Corinthians 5:7) is a necessary lesson for every Christian, but particularly those who struggle with depressive illness. Praying and pointing people to scriptures that help is part of what we do. Just because I cannot see or feel God does not mean He is not there. On the contrary, it is written, *"Never will I leave you, never will I forsake you"* (Hebrews 13:5). We need to reflect on this and say it to ourselves as a reminder that God is with us all the time. We may not know where He is, but He always knows exactly where we are.

On our courses we use the final chapter and verses in the book of Job as a guide for our prayers. Firstly, we encourage everyone to write down the things that have been said to them about their depression which have been hurtful and negative. I have observed that it is unusual for people *not* to write anything down, and this exercise can take quite a few minutes to complete, with some using two sides of the paper provided. Then, we give people permission to screw up their pieces of paper and throw them away as recognition that these are not words coming from God. Thirdly, we lead them in prayers of forgiveness for those whose words have been hurtful (just as Job had to pray for his friends). And finally, we ask God to bring healing and help into those areas affected and renew their hopes in His faithfulness to them in their situation.

I have observed some people in tears at this point, having carried much pain from the responses of others to their struggle. This part of the course takes place just after the first coffee break, at which point the atmosphere is noticeably changed. I believe that this is for two reasons. Firstly, there is the relief at discovering that this is a struggle *shared*. Depression is an isolating illness and being with others can break that sense of isolation. Secondly, the empathy in the room allows people to start talking more openly with each other. As already stated, this empathy, this common understanding, is an important factor being used by God to help communicate love and acceptance. Many reading this, I hope, will be encouraged. Your experience of depression means that God will be able to use you to help others in times to come, if He is not doing so already.

Job also says, *"Do I have the strength of stone? Is my flesh bronze? ... A despairing man should have the devotion of his friends"* (Job 6:14). If we are to tackle the very real problem of depression in godly men and women, Job's protest is one which some areas of the church may still need to hear today. At the end of the book God says to the friends:

> *So now take seven bulls and seven rams and go to my servant Job and sacrifice a burnt offering for yourselves. My servant Job will pray for you and I will accept his prayer and not deal with you according to your folly.*
>
> (Job 42:8)

Twice God says to the friends that they have not spoken "of me what is right". In matters of our witness to one another about God we must be careful not to misrepresent Him as the friends did.

A few years ago, one elderly lady in our church came up to me in tears at the end of a morning service. I had been speaking about our next course and shared a part of my own testimony. She said she realised she had judged depression in Christians too harshly in the past. Just as the 'friends' had to atone for their sin, it may be that some areas of the church will need to repent of their harsh judgements and 'wrong' words spoken, in Jesus' name.

CHAPTER FIVE

Acceptance and Permission

Scripture teaches us that Jesus meets us where we are, not in some other place. These verses from Romans 8:8 remind us of this truth: "*While we were still sinners, Christ died for us.*" We could not do anything about our situation then, and neither can we heal roots to the problems we carry, however hard we try. The Bible preacher and teacher Oswald Chambers said this:

> In spiritual issues it is customary for us to put God first, but we tend to think it is inappropriate to put Him first in the practical, everyday issues of our lives. If we have the idea that we have to put on our "spiritual face" before we can come near to God, then we will never come near to him. We must come as we are.[12]

The trouble with depression is that we feel we *should not* be there. Some would rather walk in denial than acknowledge they have a problem they cannot do anything about, especially when that problem is depression. Dr Cantopher explains why: "... on the whole the people who develop this condition have overcome every problem they have encountered in the past by extra effort. The concept of giving in to the illness is anathema."[13]

Many people with depression labour under the mistaken belief that depression is a sign of personal failure for the reasons stated by Dr Cantopher. For some the only way to alleviate this burden is to keep trying harder so they can eventually overcome and prove themselves winners instead. But the truth is that the longer a person persists in trying harder, the worse they will get, as I have found to my own personal cost. Acceptance is an important step towards help and recovery.

One woman who came to see me had her mind completely set against seeing her doctor. She came wanting prayer, but I knew that she was not well and would very likely be diagnosed with clinical depression if she went to see her doctor. But talking to her about taking this step revealed what a major hurdle it would be, for two reasons. In her own eyes, it was a sign of weakness; and for her family, a potential area of disappointment. But she *could* see herself in Dr Cantopher's typical character profile of strength, reliability and diligence. After reading it she felt more able to accept she had an illness and needed to go to the doctor. She was prescribed medication which brought her depression under control and has since said she must never let herself get ill like that again. Whilst accepting medication can be a step towards getting better, it must be remembered that for many of us there will be underlying issues which can take considerable time to resolve and heal. Part of that process is learning to accept what we *can* and what we *cannot* change.

Acceptance means we can finally acknowledge to ourselves that we need help. For the Christian it can be a time of deep spiritual growth as we have no other option than to come to Him "as we are". The Psalmist says, *"The Lord is my Shepherd"* (Psalm 23:1). While we have been 'trying harder' and trying to 'work it all out' for ourselves, there are parts of our lives that have not yet come under His Lordship and His Shepherding. The Psalmist also writes, *"he makes me lie down in green pastures"* (v2). Sometimes Jesus simply has to wait for us to reach a place where we have no choice other than to "lie down," and depression certainly takes us there. Many of us have unwittingly bought into the worldly message of self-sufficiency, and this can be replicated in church life. We must be seen to be doing well in all areas of our lives as part of our Christian witness. But the Bible conveys a different message. Our sufficiency is to be found in Christ, not ourselves. The Psalmist goes on to say, *". . . he leads me beside quiet waters; he restores my soul."* This restoration is what is needed and only God can supply it. We need to learn the appropriateness of putting Him first "in the practical everyday issues of our lives".

One of the things we all have to do when we have been ill in this way is to step back and consider what needs to change. Praying more about the "everyday issues" has shown me God's interest and answers in the minutiae of life. Priorities too have needed to change. I have had to learn to keep prioritising Christ *and* put myself further up the list of people who need my care. As my husband once said to me, "If you fall apart, we all fall apart." At that time I was under a great deal of stress at work and bringing up a young family. I was grateful for his words. They helped me to review my work situation and make some much needed changes. And I have learned to pray for wisdom in stressful situations, rather than looking for my own solutions. My faith has deepened as a consequence of having a depressive illness. But I still cannot change everything. The things I cannot change I must learn to leave with God.

On our courses we give the opportunity for people to renew their commitment to Christ. Many will acknowledge that they have been doing too much in their own strength. And many, like me, will begin to realise that God has a purpose in what has happened, and permits us to be where we are so that we can find it. God accepts depression and the people it happens to. I say this with confidence because never have I felt judged by God for my struggles with depression, but instead I have learned how to pray and ask for His help – rather than try to get around it by not mentioning it to Him. I find that God has ways through it that I can only learn about when I begin to see how He is able to meet me where I am, not where I think I should be.

In the midst of an epidemic of depressive illness we are likely to see more of it in the church. Communicating God's love and acceptance will help people to shed wrong beliefs they may be holding about themselves and their status before Him. The church's own rejection of the unhelpful questions and judgements that keep the stigma alive will help Christians find acceptance within their church family while they heal.

I believe that more positive questions for Christians to be asking are, "What value is there in being a Christian if you find yourself with a depressive illness?" and "What advantages do Christians have that non-Christians do not have?" And to borrow the Apostle Paul's expression, I would have to say, "Much in every way!" (Romans 3:2), beginning with a much better insight from the Bible about how we have been made, what might happen to cause such an illness, and the answers which, ultimately, are to be found in Christ Himself.

CHAPTER SIX

The Biblical Model

The secular world typically uses the model 'mind, body and soul' to describe our humanity. But the Bible gives us a different model to work with. It says that we have a *human spirit* as well. I have heard it said that Christians are body, soul and Holy Spirit. Modern translations of the Bible illustrate the difference by spelling the human spirit with a lower-case 's', while using a capital 'S' for the Holy Spirit. I have also heard Christians say our soul and spirit are one and the same. It is true that the two are closely linked, since we read in Hebrews 4:12 that the word of God is "*... sharper than any double-edged sword [penetrating] even to dividing soul and spirit, joints and marrow ...*" (underline added). They are close, but they too are distinct. All human beings are created in God's image: spirit, soul (thoughts and emotions) and body. Understanding the different parts of our being and how they function can give Christians a much greater insight into depressive illness and its causes. The Christian writer and counsellor Selwyn Hughes wrote:

> *According to Paul in 1 Thessalonians 5:23, there are three distinct and separate parts to our personality – 'spirit, soul and body'. Depression can be caused by a disorder in any of these areas, or from a combination of any two or all three.*[14]

We know that some depressive illnesses can have their roots in our physical being; that is to say, our *body*. We know that hormonal changes, viruses and dietary factors, for example, can be a cause. We also know that suppressed and damaged emotions in the *soul* area of our being can be a root of depression – repressed anger being an example. It is also in our *soul* that the symptoms of depression are mostly felt, in the thinking and emotional part of our being – lack of concentration, anxiety, negativity and tearfulness being common symptoms. But what of our *human spirit,* and what clues does it hold for our understanding of depressive illness?

In her book *Healing the Human Spirit,* Christian writer Ruth Hawkey says that to understand the purpose, role and function of our human spirit we need to consider what it *means* to have been created in God's own image. One example she gives is that "just as the Holy Spirit's primary job function is to communicate life to the human spirit, so in a like manner the human spirit's job function is to communicate life to our own body and soul."[15] This would seem to be confirmed in scripture with James' point about the relationship between faith and deeds: *"As the <u>body</u> without the <u>spirit</u> is dead, so faith without deeds is dead"* (James 2:26, underline added). So the first thing we learn is that our human spirit functions in our being to give *life* to the other parts.

The Bible also makes mention of *strength* to do with our human spirits. Luke, writing about John the Baptist, records that *"the child grew and became strong in spirit"* (Luke 1:80). Jesus, speaking to the crowds about John after his imprisonment, said, *"What did you go out into the desert to see? A reed swayed by the wind?"* (Matthew 11:7). John was strong in spirit and we are told that his spirit 'became' strong during his growing-up years. We may conclude, therefore, that this part of a child's development takes place alongside that of the physical, mental and emotional. In Proverbs 18:14 we read that "*a man's spirit sustains him in sickness*", indicating that one way this strength functions is to support the 'self' in times of adversity. We also experience the 'spiritual imaging' Ruth Hawkey talks about in other key areas, such as in creativity, joy and identity. In the opening chapter of the Book of Genesis we read,

> *In the beginning God created the heavens and the earth. Now the earth was formless and empty, darkness was over the surface of the deep and the Spirit of God was hovering over the waters.*
> (Genesis 1:2).

As anyone who dances, is musical, paints, carves, writes, knits or sews will testify, the act of creating can be deeply satisfying and results in much appreciation of what has been created, just as "*God saw all that he had made, and it was very good*" (Genesis 1:31).

In one of the acclaimed TED Talks, Dr Ken Robinson criticises education systems for educating children out of their creative capacity and teaching them that it is wrong to make mistakes. It has, he says, become the worst thing now in schools (and in the workplace) to make mistakes and we have started to create a stigma around them.[16] This may explain some of the stress being experienced by so many young people today. If we are suppressing an important part of what they have to offer *and* creating the capacity to fear failure in areas where they may not feel as gifted, stress and tension would seem to be an inevitable outcome. It is interesting to note that creativity is used extensively in therapy and can help people discover or rediscover the deep satisfaction of being able to create something. This ability to create and appreciate bypasses our thoughts and emotions to somewhere much deeper within and can be extremely helpful and healing to people who are depressed.

Our human spirit is also that part of us where we may experience deep *joy*. Luke records Mary's response to Elizabeth's greeting of blessing on her and her unborn baby: *"My soul glorifies the Lord, and <u>my spirit rejoices</u> in God my Saviour"* (Luke 1:40-47, underline added).

Ruth Hawkey defines our human spirit as being "that part of us which makes us completely different from every other person; it is the essential 'you' which is totally unique and special."[17] It is where our identity is located and would explain why, when a person is rejected, shamed or humiliated, the consequences are so deeply felt. It also raises further questions for consideration: What of the person whose human spirit has never been allowed to grow and flourish, where the "essential you" inside them has received the frequent communication that it needs something other than itself, some additional authentication to give it value and worth? What of the human spirit that has been met with disapproval, harsh treatment, neglect or abuse? The answer is that under these circumstances the human spirit may be crushed or broken and unable to fulfil its God-given function and purpose. People who have been damaged like that will have to work very hard in life, producing for themselves the kinds of comforts, pleasures, purposes and affirmations they need, to feed back to themselves that which is missing through harm or neglect. The Bible has something to say about human spirits that have been *crushed* or, even worse, completely *broken*.

CHAPTER SEVEN

A Crushed Spirit

A crushed or broken spirit will be unable to perform its function of communicating life, comfort and strength to the soul and body and may result in some wanting to give up on life altogether. It is no longer the place where joy is experienced, and creative desires may also diminish as people no longer see the point. Those with a crushed or broken spirit will be living with an invisible disability which will need sensitive and considerate care to nurture them back to strength and hope. So how does this kind of damage happen?

The Bible teaches that one reason a person's spirit can become *crushed* is to do with *words*. We read in Proverbs 15:4 *"a deceitful tongue crushes the spirit"* and in Proverbs 18:21 *"The tongue has the power of life and death."* Many will be crushed in their spirits because of hurtful words spoken against them, especially when they come from parents or those in authority. At this point, self-worth and validation, in particular, may be undermined – as I was to discover in the unintended consequences of my mother's words to me when I was about three years old.

There were only fourteen months between me and my older brother and he had just angrily thrown a toy wooden train at me. My head was bleeding and I had asked my mum why my brother hated me so much. She said, "It is because you have come into the family too early." Her words gave me a deep pain inside, much worse than the pain in my head. I realise now that they embedded within me a deep sense of rejection, and the 'you' in her statement made me feel that I was somehow responsible for my mistimed arrival. As a consequence, I grew up with a great need to validate my own existence. Also, when other difficulties came my way I formed the belief that bad things would happen to me because I should not really be here. Not only did I lose spiritual strength, I did not develop any defences or strategies to deal with adverse situations, presuming them to be my lot in life. Prayers and scriptures like this one from Isaiah have helped me to heal and reverse the negative effect those words had on me. *"I took you from the ends of the earth, from its farthest corners I called you. I said, 'You are my servant'; I have chosen you and not rejected you"* (Isaiah 41:9).

When a person's spirit has been crushed through words of rejection, abuse or unkindness, it will inevitably shrink back and need to protect itself from further hostility. When this happens the mind will need to take control, working out how to avoid further pain and do what is necessary to feel better. Life then becomes more about *doing* than *being,* and this may hold a vital clue to understanding why, under these circumstances, some people become clinically depressed. The effort of living simply becomes too hard. The stresses, worries and troubles of modern-day living begin to add further burdens on an already damaged spirit and overwrought mind. The result, as Dr Cantopher writes, is like when "you put 18 amps through a 13-amp fuse – there is only one result. Stress-related depressive illness is essentially a blown fuse."[18] And the root to it may be a crushing of a person's spirit at some point earlier in their lives. It may also well be that the crushing of a person's spirit is the reason too for the lowered serotonin levels in the brain, since, in Proverbs 17:22, we read that *"a crushed spirit dries up the bones."* Clearly a crushed spirit has consequences in the physical part of our being, as it is no longer able to bring life to the other parts.

We can also be crushed by the burdens placed on us by others. Ruth Hawkey writes that "One of the main causes of a crushed spirit is inappropriate burden bearing," and that "many people are called upon to walk through life with responsibilities which are far too onerous for their age or experience."[19] This also may account for the increase in depressive illness in the younger generation. In an article for The Independent in 2016, Geraldine Bedell asks the question, "How has society managed to produce a generation of teenagers in which mental health problems are so prevalent?" Quoting the work of William Davies in his book *The Happiness Industry,* she writes that Davies presents "evidence to demonstrate that strongly materialistic and competitive values lead to higher levels of mental distress". Bedell writes that for young people, "exams, parental expectations, and social media are part of what is becoming an epidemic of stress and unhappiness in the younger generation."[20]

Even worse than a crushed spirit is one that has been completely broken. This may happen for a number of reasons, such as loss, fear and control by others. A person with a broken spirit will need a lot of help, nurturing, comfort and time to recover a sense of well-being, perspective and purpose.

CHAPTER EIGHT

A Broken Spirit

Job, in his own distress, says, *"My spirit is broken, my days are cut short, the grave awaits me"* (Job 17:10). His experience is one of *loss,* a known factor in the cause of depression. As Job's story demonstrates, any loss – family, status, wealth, health – can all be factors which can break a person's spirit and cause them to become depressed. Looking back, I realise that the divorce of my parents was when I began to really struggle in life. The breakdown of family relationships and the loss of our family home and the life we once had brought sorrow, insecurity and fearfulness about life in general. Not knowing how to process any of it, I now realise, led to feelings of isolation and depression.

We have had many people on our courses who have shared their own personal stories of loss. For some, grief itself has been stifled and stalled because there was no permission to talk about it, as was the case with one young woman whose mother had died when she was a little girl. Her father had removed all photographs of her and she had not been allowed to talk about her mother at home. Being with others who can empathise with the pain of loss can bring a level of comfort to a broken spirit, especially when it feels that God is a long way away.

Fear can also break a person's spirit, creating another reason why a person might want to give up on life. In

1 Kings 19:3 we read that Elijah *"was afraid and ran for his life"* following Jezebel's threats against him. He eventually lay down under a broom tree, *"praying that he might die"* (v4). Many people with a depressive illness will find that fear and anxiety will cause them to feel the kind of panic that sets in motion the fight or flight response. Problems that seem unsolvable give potential for fear to become overwhelming when a person no longer knows what to do. When their spirit has been crushed or broken, and the mind no longer has the answers, the body is all that is left and under these circumstances 'flight' is the only thing left to do.

When our first child was born it was with a serious life-threatening condition, requiring immediate life-saving surgery. The surgery to repair his oesophagus and trachea were successful, but we were also told there were no guarantees. Many children did not make it after these operations; thirty years previously, none would have made it at all. It was still relatively early days for this kind of surgery. Being cocooned in the hospital environment day by day for two months gave me a level of security and helped me deal with the 'one step forward and two steps back' of his recovery. I longed for the day when we could eventually bring him home. That day finally came when he was eight weeks old. But with him still only weighing 6lbs and without the safety net of the hospital, I was fearful of what could happen. During his first year we had countless emergency visits to the hospital with many life-saving interventions. Whilst out with a friend for a meal during this time, I experienced the first of many panic attacks, which created a new level of fear, since each brought with it a feeling that I might die. Afraid that this might happen when I was out, I stopped going out and spent much of our son's first year at home, unable to find my way back to any sense of stability and normality.

I was in that place of brokenness where my mind and emotions were overwrought and my body was persistently giving me the signal to run. It was a few months after our son's first birthday and further surgery that a friend shared her faith with me and I then committed my life to Christ. The panic attacks ceased immediately and I felt a complete peace about our son's future too. He is grown up now and has just become a father himself, and I am thankful every day that God brought us through such a difficult time. As He has worked with me over the years, the fear 'mountain' has diminished and I look back at those times and wonder where I would be today if I had not found Him then.

Fear can overwhelm the godly as well as the ungodly. Living under constant fear and anxiety is extremely exhausting and debilitating. God's answer for Elijah, to begin with, was sustenance and rest. Today the fear of failure for many is a driving force creating a need to perform and achieve as if our very lives depend on it. For those who are caught up in this kind of turmoil, illness itself may enforce the rest which is needed for recovery and a fresh perspective. Antidepressants may be part of the 'sustenance' needed to restore the depleted levels of serotonin so that a broken spirit can begin to recover and an anxious mind can rest. Then, when a person is stronger, the roots to the fears can be challenged and dealt with.

Control, manipulation and domination by others can also lead to a person's spirit being broken, because they are being *overruled* as a person in their own right. This overruling of another's choices and decisions is not in keeping with the way God works with us. Jesus says, *"If anyone chooses to do God's will"* (John 7:17, underline added), so choice is important. If that is taken away from us and we become manipulated and dominated by the will of others, damage is the inevitable consequence. Oswald Chambers said, "If one rules another by saying, 'you must do this' and 'you will do that' he breaks the human spirit..."[21]

The word 'trespass' came to mean a lot to me as the Lord was teaching me these things. Having had a very controlling upbringing, I realised that I had not really ever learned to make choices for myself and consequently found it difficult to find my own voice and know what to do in many situations I encountered. I did not recognise when I was being manipulated and often carried feelings of guilt when I felt a reluctance to do what another person wanted. When you are on the receiving end of this kind of control it does not feel good and it does not feel right, but you do not know why. The word *trespass* gave me an insight into why this was the case. In the older translation of the Lord's prayer *trespass* is used in the place of debt or sin: *"Forgive us our trespasses as we forgive those who trespass against us."* I began to see that control, manipulation and domination are all forms of trespassing. It is a crossing of boundaries into the territory of another person's life and that's why it does not feel good.

As I was learning about this I began to see how much of my life had been controlled, and it was a real revelation. God was teaching me that He did not want me to continue to be controlled in ways that I had been, and He wanted me to find my own voice and rebuff any attempts to 'trespass'. Following this I had an amusing interaction with my husband in a supermarket. I was about to push our trolley towards something I wanted to buy on our shopping list and he told me to go and get something else first. I said, "I will get that in a minute." He told me again. I said, "No.

Stop telling me what to do." We ended up having something of an argument in the middle of the supermarket aisle. On another day it would not have mattered, but on that day it did. I explained to him afterwards that God was teaching me about control and it was good to have an open and frank discussion about it.

Nevertheless, I have found that walking away from being controlled by others has taken time. I have had to learn strategies when talking to those who would want to impose their thoughts over mine. I am less timid and have grown in confidence, but find that nearly thirty years later, the call is still to be 'strong' and 'courageous'. As God calls me to new things I still wonder sometimes how on earth I am going to do them. But then I find His strength is right there with me and I need not have worried at all, not in the slightest.

There may still be much that we do not understand about our human spirits, but one thing we do know is that the Bible says, *"The Lord is close to the broken-hearted and saves those who are crushed in spirit"* (Psalm 34:18). God has a special interest in those who are damaged in this way. As Jesus began His ministry to the crowds He started by saying, *"Blessed are the poor in spirit, for theirs is the kingdom of heaven. Blessed are those who mourn, for they will be comforted"* (Matthew 5:3-4). And His answer for those who have been broken or crushed, wearied or burdened is simply, *"Come to me"* (Matthew 11:28).

CHAPTER NINE

"Come to Me"

*Come to me, all you who are weary and
burdened, and I will give you rest. Take my yoke
upon you and learn from me, for I am gentle and
humble in heart, and you will find rest for your
souls. For my yoke is easy and my burden is light.*

(Matthew 11:28-30)

The pressures and pace of life today mean that many are
suffering the wearying effects of stress in unprecedented
ways and are in much need of the *rest* being promised here.
Jesus says a lot of things in this scripture which are worth
pausing to consider. The invitation is to "Come" and find His
"rest". When I first came to Him and gave my life to Him in a
prayer of commitment, it was with great relief that I realised I
did not have to 'do life' on my own anymore. I felt a peace and
a rest from much inner turmoil and knew I had come 'home'.
However, I have needed to come back to this scripture again
and again as I've realised that was only the beginning and
God had much more for me to learn, especially about being
'burdened' and how this was a component factor in my own
struggle with depressive illness.

On our courses we teach about *burdens* because that
is the language that Jesus uses. We use bags loaded

down with something heavy to show the reality of what many are carrying with them on the inside: fear, control, worries, troubles, stress, anxiety and so on. We explain that depression itself can become just another burden to be carried on top of the many others we may be carrying, but not necessarily recognising. Learning that God *is not* expecting us to carry these burdens can make all the difference and help to recover a struggling faith.

The stigma of depression, which firmly places the responsibility to do better on ourselves, is challenged by these words, "Come to me." As we do, we will find Him beginning the work of reversing our preconceptions about our status before Him when we have this illness.

But it is difficult to come to Him if we have begun to believe ourselves to be separated. Looking through the Bible for some encouragement one day, I read these verses:

> *I will give you the treasures of darkness, riches stored in secret places so that you may know that I am the Lord, the God of Israel who calls you by name.*
>
> (Isaiah 45:3).

As I began to meditate on these words, my perspective began to change. They conveyed to me a deeply personal message of hope and reassurance that, although I could not see Him, He could see me. He knew where I was and what He was going to do. There was the promise of something to be gained, new things He wanted to give me, and most importantly, I would come to know Him better. This had a profound effect on my understanding of how God uses what we go through for our ultimate benefit, even depression. That is not to say that He gave me a depressive illness so that He could do all this. It is to say that, in a world that has fallen from grace, He was willing to meet with me and recover what had been broken and what had been lost, without judgement and with great kindness. It is an encouragement that I am keen to pass on to others, and we explore Isaiah 45:3 together on our courses. I no longer hide my depression away, and as a leader at Farnham Baptist Church have been willing to stand at the front to talk about depression and the courses we run, and invite others to come along and find this same encouragement. I can say with great conviction that God is for me in depression and not against me, and He wants me to bring the whole *burden* of it to Him.

When we look at the verses from Matthew together on our courses we invite people to think about how easy or difficult they find it to surrender their burdens to God. Most of us would agree that it is not easy. Even when we do, we have a tendency to take things back to ourselves to try and work it all out in our own strength – which is why some of us have become ill in the first place. Being together helps us to see that we all struggle in a similar way and we can genuinely help and encourage one another to take new steps of faith with God. We need to persevere if we want to participate in the 'rest' being offered. Not just any rest, but rest for our souls – a mental and emotional rest from the struggles of the world. And Jesus mentions it *twice*, so it must be important! As we begin to line our lives up with Him in this way, surrendering our whole selves to Him, we can begin to *learn* from Jesus the things He wants to teach us. At this point on our courses some people want to re-commit their lives to Christ. You can use the following prayer, if you feel prompted to do the same.

Lord Jesus

I realise that I have been trying to do too much in my own strength and am struggling now under the weight of many burdens. I turn back to You and gratefully surrender my life back into Your hands. Please fill me again with Your Holy Spirit so that I can start afresh and learn how to walk in step with You.

Amen

CHAPTER TEN

"Take my yoke upon you"

Some years ago, I was reflecting on how the first day of one of our courses had gone, in particular the session we had done on Matthew 11:28-30. I felt the Lord's prompting to say something more about the verses which speak of being *yoked* to Him, especially as *yoking* is not a word used much today in everyday language. So, what is meant by 'yoking', and more specifically, what does it mean to take Jesus' yoke upon us?

Traditionally the word 'yoke' is used in farming to describe a heavy wooden bar used to join oxen for the purpose of ploughing fields in pairs. This is a *physical* joining or connecting of one animal to another in an obvious way and for an obvious purpose. In human terms we are yoked by the invisible ties we form in our relationships with one another: parent/child, husband/wife, doctor/patient, teacher/pupil, boss/employee, friendships, and so forth. All these God gave for our good and many are blessed through them. But, as we are warned in scripture, not all relationships will be good and some ties may cause us to take on a wooden heaviness like that which joins the oxen together.

The apostle Paul had to counsel the Corinthian and Galatian churches to be careful in this respect, saying, *"Do not be yoked with unbelievers. For what do righteousness and wickedness have in common?"* (2 Corinthians 6:14). To the

Galatians he wrote that they must resist those who would bring false teaching into the church: *"Stand firm then and do not let yourselves be burdened again by a yoke of slavery"* (Galatians 5:1). Some yokes, therefore, can do a great deal of harm and many who have been ill with depression may need help in this area.

On one of our courses I met a lady whose life was being undermined by fear and anxiety. We prayed together, asking for God to set her free and bring release. At one of our support group meetings she shared that the problem had started during a consultation with an optician. She was diagnosed with the beginnings of a cataract and left the appointment afraid of losing her eyesight. She then went to another optician where she was greatly reassured, but the anxiety remained. The situation was lifted to God once again in prayer. At the next meeting she came back and reported that she had felt prompted and emboldened to go back to the original optician and asked to be removed from their mailing list. This had the immediate effect of removing much of her anxiety since every communication brought with it a fearful reminder of that initial consultation. God had begun to answer our prayers by giving her the courage to break that original connection, where the fear had started.

About a year ago I was challenged by God about re-connecting with an old 'friend' on social media. This was a childhood friend whom I had known from nursery school days and we had spent much time together until we were about eleven and about to go to grammar school. At this point she had made it clear that she did not want to continue our friendship. In later years our paths crossed with shared friends, but I always sensed her resentment at my being present at any get-togethers. But surely,

I thought, God would want me to be her friend. However, as I felt challenged about it, I took her off my list of 'friends'. Shortly afterwards He began to uncover some hurt feelings from her earlier rejection and began to heal me from them. On my part, I needed to forgive her and then let her go. I began to realise that a consequence of that earlier experience was the undermining of my confidence in making new friends, and I had not committed to a 'best' friend like that since. These relational ties are profoundly important to our sense of well-being and can impact the way in which we meet with Jesus – most especially when we have been hurt by those in *authority* over us.

When we become a Christian we become yoked to Jesus, and for many this will be a wonderful experience, as it was with me – for about three days. I enjoyed three wonderful days of experiencing the love He had for me, a peace which I had never experienced before and a rest from much inner turmoil. After that, I began to feel empty and fear seemed to take over. I started to wonder what I might have done to spoil it all. I understand now that part of the problem was rooted in a childhood experience with my father when I was about seven.

We were outside sweeping up leaves together. I was excited to share in this task with him – but I did something wrong. I accidentally messed up the pile of leaves we had raked together before he could gather it up. But because it made him laugh, I did it again, thinking it was becoming a game to enjoy together. Unfortunately, I did it one too many times. In anger he picked me up and threw me over his knees and began to spank me very hard. I remember trying to cry but no sound came out. The beating did not stop until my mother, alerted by a neighbour, came out to intervene. A few days later I was taken to see our family doctor as I was limping quite badly, but I was not allowed to say what had happened. The doctor thought my leg might have been fractured and I was bandaged from the thigh to the ankle for some time. I told him I had fallen off my bike. I did not want to get my dad into trouble. I loved him but I also feared his anger and what he might do. The physical wounds healed but the consequences remained deep inside as anxiety rooted in fearful expectations.

It took quite a while for me to learn that God was different to my father, who had modelled to me a type of authority which I assumed would be replicated in all authority figures. And it took time to walk away from the many rules I believed I needed to live by in order to avoid the ultimate consequence of harsh punishment.

So deeply were these rules ingrained into me that in my early years of being a Christian I spent many hours studying the Bible in search of the things that might make God angry so that I could avoid doing them. But even so, I was sure that somewhere along the line I would end up having got it wrong and would need to be punished. I agonized over the 'unforgivable sin' spoken about by Jesus, believing myself to be in danger of committing it even though I was not really sure what it was. But it held me in a place of fear since, in my mind, it was the one thing that would make God angry and ultimately reject me. It took a long time to accept that I was beyond that danger, since the scripture refers to those who, having spent their whole lives rejecting the promptings of the Holy Spirit to reveal Christ to them, ultimately close the door forever on any hope of forgiveness. Thankfully, I am no longer in such a place of fear. He who is "gentle and humble in heart" said, ". . . *do not fear, for I am with you; do not be dismayed, for I am your God. I will strengthen you and help you; I will uphold you with my righteous right hand"* (Isaiah 41:10). In other words, what I could not do for myself, that part of me that was holding back, He would help me with so that I could move on from such a place. And He has. Today, nearly thirty years on, faith has replaced fear, just as He said it would when He gave me this scripture to hold onto*: "For I am the Lord, your God, who takes hold of your right hand and says to you, Do not fear, I will help you"* (Isaiah 41:13).

Several people who have come on our courses have encountered harshness through authority figures in their lives which has left a lasting impact on them and their ability to let Jesus into their problems. Some will struggle with never feeling quite 'good enough', or being enslaved by feelings of guilt, fear and shame. Some will keep confessing the same things over and over again, never feeling that they are really forgiven. For others there may have been abuse or harsh treatment. Some, like me, may have begun their Christian walk with great joy, having 'tasted' that the Lord is good, but found it difficult to progress much further. There can be a fearfulness that holds people back, with past experiences signalling the need to be careful, even with Jesus, just in case. Being yoked to Jesus means He can teach us that His ways are different to those who have been overly harsh – especially when we have encountered that harshness more than once.

I remember being frozen in fear on another occasion by my father's anger. I had drunk some milk and not left enough for him to have a cup of tea. As my brother and I sat watching the television he came into the lounge angrily demanding to know who had drunk the milk. I could not own up even though I wanted to. It has been wonderful to learn that God does not use that kind of fear to teach or discipline us. On the contrary, *"perfect love drives out fear"*

(1 John 4:18). And love, I have learned, is a much better teacher than fear. I recall having a conversation with a Christian friend who said that children want to be able to own up to their mistakes but, as parents, we have to create the right environment in which they can do it.

As a new Christian, I had a wonderful opportunity to put this lesson into practice. It was a little while before Christmas and I had bought some chocolate foil-wrapped Father Christmas figures for our children, then aged seven and three, to decorate the Christmas tree and to enjoy on Christmas Day. Leaving them to it, I went to do something else in the kitchen. When I went back into the lounge there was a trail of silver foil and several missing Father Christmases. I gently asked which of them had left the wrappings and eaten the chocolate. Both denied it. So I said that I wanted whoever it was to own up to me; they would not be in trouble and they did not have to tell me straight away, but I did want whoever it was to tell me the truth. I then went back into the kitchen to carry on with what I had been doing and forgot all about it. Some while later, I went back into the lounge and noticed that our three-year-old daughter was still curled up in the same ball, on the same chair, as when I had left. All of a sudden she said, "It was me, Mummy." It was clearly a relief for her to be able to say it. She uncurled herself and I gave her a hug to let her know it was alright, she was forgiven and I was not cross. She knew she had done something wrong and realised she felt better once she owned up. She also learned about consequences. In this case it was that her brother was allowed to eat the rest of the chocolates with my full permission since she had already had her share. It was a gentle lesson that I was able to teach her and one for which I take no credit. Without a doubt, had Jesus not intervened in my life when He did, I would have repeated the patterns of behaviour learned in my own childhood – and hated myself for it.

Sometimes Jesus Himself needs to break the heavy dysfunctional yokings that tie us to our past and hold us back from coming to Him with confidence and freedom. In the book of Hosea we read, *"I led them with cords of human kindness, with ties of love. I lifted the yoke from their neck and bent down to feed them"* (Hosea 11:4). And where authority figures have been harsh, rejecting, abusive and difficult, it is important to begin to learn and embrace the truth that Jesus is not like them. He says, *"Take my yoke upon you and learn from me, for I am gentle and humble in heart and you will find rest for your souls"* (Matthew 11:29).

Whatever our experiences, Jesus makes it plain in His teaching to His disciples that the old associations between authority, servanthood and slavery are changed under the new covenant. This helps us to understand what He means when He goes on to say, *"my yoke is easy"* (Matthew 11:30).

CHAPTER ELEVEN

"My yoke is easy"

For the reasons mentioned in the previous chapter, notions of an *easy* yoke with someone in authority over us may be difficult to grasp when there are no concrete terms of reference in our experience. There are many reasons why people will find it hard to draw near to God and there are many scriptures which reassure us of His faithfulness and gentleness to help us overcome them: *"Do not be afraid; you will not suffer shame"* (Isaiah 54:4), *"A bruised reed he will not break"* (Isaiah 42:3), and Jesus' own words, *"I am gentle and humble in heart"* (Matthew 11:29). Unlike human beings, God is also reassuringly consistent, as James says, and *"does not change like shifting shadows"* (James 1:17).

In addition to these reassurances, there is something else to be understood about Jesus' authority from His teaching to His disciples. He says to them, *"I no longer call you servants... instead I have called you friends"* (John 15:15). The dynamics of the traditional authoritative relationship between a King and his people are significantly changed in these words. He is both Lord and King, but He invites us into *friendship* with Him, to be involved with Him in carrying out His plans and purposes.

More than that, we are also to understand that He does not want us to feel like *slaves* either. Paul, writing to the Galatians, says, *"you are no longer a slave but a son"*

(Galatians 4:7). We are now part of God's family with an inheritance *"that can never perish, spoil or fade"* (1 Peter 1:4) and we are sealed with His Holy Spirit for the day of redemption (Ephesians 4:30). Paul says, *"it is for freedom that Christ has set us free"* (Galatians 5:1). This freedom is about knowing that our sins are forgiven, our mistakes are redeemable and that the 'rules' enslaving our old lives no longer apply.

Jesus also wants to help us in the whole area of relationships where betrayal, rejection, abandonment, neglect and loss have created discouragement and vulnerability. Many of us will need to be reminded and reassured about His faithfulness in all circumstances. One scripture that was on my mind all the time as a new Christian was, *"Never will I leave you, never will I forsake you"* (Hebrews 13:5). I used to wonder why, not yet understanding how past experiences had influenced my ongoing struggles and difficulties. I realise now that it was a truth that He wanted me to grasp and walk in because He knew how much I feared rejection. As Jesus prepares His disciples for what is to come, He says, *"I will not leave you as orphans, I will come to you"* (John 14:18). It is a forever relationship where nothing can separate us from Him, as Paul testified to the Roman church:

> *For I am convinced that neither death nor life,*
> *neither angels nor demons, neither the present*
> *nor the future, nor any powers, neither height nor*
> *depth, nor anything else in all creation, will be*
> *able to separate us from the love of God that is in*
> *Christ Jesus our Lord.*

(Romans 8:38-39)

Jesus says that we are His friends, His sons and daughters, and His commitment to us is covenanted and eternal. In other words, His 'yoke' is easy for all who choose to wear it. But Jesus still has not finished everything He wants to say to us in these verses in Matthew 11:28-30. The final thing He needs to teach us is in these words, *"my burden is light"* (v30). Christians with depression are typically very good at carrying burdens of all kinds and we need to understand more about this *light burden* that Jesus is talking about.

CHAPTER TWELVE

"My burden is light"

As we recover from depression, it is important to let Jesus help us set new boundaries and recognise the things we need to let go. Some Christians will be trying to serve in ways they are not gifted for. As a new Christian, I spent many a Sunday concerned that I was not doing enough for the Lord in the area of evangelism. But evangelism, I now realise, is not my gifting. Jesus said to His disciples, *"... you will receive power when the Holy Spirit comes and you will be my <u>witnesses</u> ..."* (Acts 1:8, underline added). As Christians, we are all called to be His witnesses, but that witness will be expressed differently in different people, according to how He has gifted them. Ephesians 4:11 says, *"It was he who gave some to be apostles, some to be prophets, some to be evangelists and some to be pastors and teachers"*.

I can and do share my faith whenever God gives me the opportunity, but my gifts are more pastorally focused and I love to pray with people. We are all gifted and we are all gifted differently. It is important that we do not burden one another with a 'one size fits all' approach in our witness for the Lord or privilege some gifts above others and convey a sense of unequal significances in our service to Him. As it is written, *"if the whole body were an ear, where would the sense of smell be?"* (1 Corinthians 12:17).

Sometimes our Christian burden is too heavy because we do not know how to say 'no'. Learning to say 'no' will be hard for someone who has depression. Their diligence and sense of responsibility makes it difficult. They will need to be told that it is not just okay to say 'no', but it is vital that they do – if they want to get well and avoid becoming ill again. The problem for us all is that lives are getting busier and busier and the church is no exception. As he was about to leave our fellowship to take up a calling elsewhere, one of our ministers at Farnham Baptist Church reflected on the many good things that were going on in our church. It was a busy place. But he also cautioned us to check, from time to time, whether we were busy for the Lord; or just busy.

At other times we may need to put down the thing we have been doing for God. Some ministries come to a natural end and it will be hard work to keep them going. Sometimes God wants to give us new direction and stretch our faith in different areas. We need the Lord's wisdom and help in such times, to be able to put things down and move on to new opportunities. I have had to learn that sometimes it is only when I put something down that God will bring someone else forward to pick it up. This has helped remove any sense of personal guilt that somehow I would be letting people down when I could not continue with something I had been doing. Jesus says to each of us, *"my yoke is easy and my burden is light..."* (Matthew 11:30). The Message translates it like this:

> *Walk with me and work with me – watch how I do it. Learn the unforced rhythms of grace. I will not lay anything heavy or ill-fitting on you. Keep company with me and you'll learn to live freely and lightly.*[22]

This is a different way of life than most of us with depressive illness will have been living. When we have been broken down by life we have to take stock and work out what to do differently. These verses in Matthew can be summed up in three words: Come, Rest and Learn. Depression creates a forced opportunity to change and live differently. God wants us to take that opportunity to learn what it means to let Him be the One to show the way forward. For many of us this will mean learning what He does and does not want us to be *responsible* for.

CHAPTER THIRTEEN

Burden-bearing and Responsibility

As we have seen from Dr Cantopher's profile, people with depression are good at picking up responsibility. "He or she is strong, reliable, diligent, with a strong conscience and sense of responsibility . . ."[23] The 'sense of responsibility' being described means that we can be very good at picking up the burden of other people's problems but not be very good at giving attention to our own. What many of us need help with is recognising what God does and does not want us to be *responsible* for.

In her book, *A Child No More*, Mary Pytches writes of the importance of discerning where our responsibilities lie if we are to mature as Christians. She writes:

> For many reasons it is important that this discipline of taking responsibility should become an essential part of our lives. No-one can mature without it. If a person can learn to identify how much responsibility is his, pick that up and leave what is not, he will mature with rapidity. It is a vital discipline for growth.[24]

I want to highlight two key areas where a Christian with a depressive illness may find the lines somewhat blurred and confusing in this respect. The first is that of the need to take 'control' in all situations and at all times. This means *taking responsibility for things we are not supposed to*. The other area is that of 'blame' towards those who have hurt or damaged us in some way. This means *not taking responsibility for things we are supposed to*. Both need some explanation to show why these can be present in our lives and why they may be hindering our growth as Christians.

Control

On one level, we all know what control is and the damage it does. Many of us will know people whom we would call 'control freaks', and we may smugly thank God that we are not like that. Or we may recognise it in ourselves and happily tell others that we are the control freaks and laugh it off as one of our many funny quirks. Or we may not recognise it at all until it begins to reveal itself as a coping mechanism for life that is no longer working – such as when we begin to struggle with a depressive illness. For people like this, becoming ill *and* realising that all coping mechanisms have begun to fail can take them into an additional crisis. What had seemed to be a strength to themselves and others has revealed itself to be an illusion, a building on sand.

Many will have developed this type of control as a coping mechanism in an attempt to keep their own world safe and secure. The root is very often to do with trauma and fear. For some, it is a consequence of the need to take on responsibility for their own well-being from an early age when kindness and love were in short supply. For others, it may have been learned from parents, and for them, it will be a 'normal' part of human behaviour.

As I sat in a counselling session one day, the subject of control kept coming up. I realised I did not really know what it was. Seeking clarification, I asked the question, "What is the difference between control and leadership?" It was explained to me that a good leader will be able to trust those around them to do what has been asked of them. A controlling person will not be able to do that. They will need to micro-manage every detail to ensure everything is done 'right'. The key word was 'trust'.

If we are to grow through the negative experience of depression where control has been one of our coping mechanisms in life, we need, with God's help, to learn how to trust in Christ more and more. As Jesus was preparing His disciples for what was to come He said to them, *"Do not let your hearts be troubled, do not be afraid; trust in me"* (John 14:27). We too need to learn how to put these words into practice so that we can lean on Jesus and not on our own resources in times of crisis. The truth is that when we are troubled we tend to take matters into our own hands. Many people will have become ill with depression simply because they are picking up responsibility for too many things. The invitation to the 'weary and burdened' is to come to Jesus, to start bringing the burdens and problems to the cross, to start praying instead of striving.

Understanding more about control has been a real eye-opener for me and, over time, I began to see how much control I was bringing to my own life and relationships. Over-thinking and over-planning all the time causes a great deal of mental strain and I did not want to be spinning all those plates anymore. It is hard work keeping them all up in the air and control is not good for relationships either. More than that, it halts our growth as Christians. Oswald Chambers said:

> The greatest spiritual blessing we receive is when we come to the knowledge that we are destitute. Until we get there, our Lord is powerless. He can do nothing for us as long as we think we are sufficient in and of ourselves.[25]

Control is our attempt to run our own lives and is contrary to the Lordship of Christ. For those reading this who feel led to do so, here is a prayer to help you bring the problem of control to God in confession and repentance:

Lord Jesus

Thank You that you have called me into a relationship with You. I am sorry for the ways in which I have still tried to control my own life, my problems and struggles, and not allowed You to be Lord in those areas. I bring my whole self to You now and ask You to be Lord in every area. I particularly bring to You my struggle with depression and pray that You will be the One to lead me and guide me to the help and answers I need.

I am sorry too for the ways in which I have tried to control others and trespassed into their lives with my own agenda for working out their problems and their struggles. Help me to pray for Your wisdom and guidance in their situations and step back and let You be the One to bring the solutions they need.

Thank You that Your burden for me is light and I pray that You will continue to teach me where my responsibilities are and where they are not, for Your glory and not my own.
In Your name
Amen

Blame

The second area of error is to do with blaming others. When we have been hurt, it is all too easy to remain in a place of blame towards others for the pain we have experienced. We may recognise this in our anger and feelings of resentment towards certain people. Our 'worldly' reasoning tells us that since the pain was inflicted by another, we really need *them* to put matters right with *us*. The faulty assumption is that we cannot change or do anything because someone else is responsible for our problems. But the Bible says the opposite. Explicit in these words of scripture, "in your anger do not sin" (Ephesians 4:26), is the truth that my anger is mine and no-one else's, and it is up to me how I deal with it. Recognising where our responsibilities lay in this respect is the first step to resolving our issues with others, especially when we find anger, resentment and bitterness to be a growing problem in our lives.

At a seminar at New Wine in the early 1990s, I heard Mary Pytches use an example from everyday life to explain this point. She said that every morning for most of her married life she'd had the same argument with her husband about leaving his laundry on the bedroom floor instead of putting it in the linen basket in the bathroom. One day, she told him she did not understand why he should have such a problem with this. At which point, she felt the conviction of the Holy Spirit that her husband did not have a problem with the situation at all. She was the one who was angry day by day. It dawned on her that, this being the case, she could take responsibility то find a solution. And the answer was simple. She moved the linen basket from the bathroom into the bedroom and the problem was solved.

Recognising whose problem is whose is key if we are to work towards finding solutions with God's help. Taking responsibility for our problems, however they got there, and forgiving those who caused them, is the only way He offers us His help to move on. When we blame we are in a passive place where nothing changes and nothing gets resolved. Worse than that we, albeit unwittingly, become like the unmerciful servant in Matthew 18:21-35, waiting for a debt to be repaid, and are thus found ourselves to be at fault before God.

As I was listening to Mary Pytches speak on this subject, I felt the conviction that this was me. I knew that I had harboured much bitterness and resentment towards my parents for my struggles in life. When I had become a Christian I knew this was not right and forgave them as much as I could and repented. But I also knew I was not free and still carried much of the pain and hurt from their divorce and the breakdown of our relationships. At the end of her talk, I responded to the invitation to go forward for prayer. When asked why I would like prayer I managed only a few words, "I blame my parents..." I did not get as far as explaining why. As soon as the words were spoken I broke down in tears and I could feel a warmth go through my body. This went on for several minutes. I left that session exhausted but realised that I had experienced what it says in 1 John 1:9, that *"if we confess our sins he is faithful and just to forgive us our sins and purify us from all unrighteousness"* (underline added). As a direct consequence, I knew I did not carry the resentment and bitterness anymore and, more than that, I also knew I did not want to go down the pathway of blame ever again. The people whom I had held responsible for my pain had not changed at all. But I was different and enabled to move on.

I had done what I could to turn round in repentance, but I had never understood the need for confession like that. I do now and it is a lesson I have never forgotten. When we take responsibility for our problems *however they got there*, willing to forgive and release those who have hurt us, God is able to bring help and healing to us. This also taught me that forgiveness is primarily for my benefit, not theirs. Many find it difficult to forgive because it seems as though what they have suffered is being ignored and the person is 'getting away with it'. But that is not what forgiveness does. They are not getting away with what they have done. God will deal with them and judge them accordingly. I, on the other hand, when I am prepared to do things His way, can find God's renewed strength to walk away from difficult and hurtful experiences.

Understanding that my hurt feelings and emotions belong to me has helped me to address conflict in a much more positive way. Instead of letting hurt feelings fester by not addressing them, I have learnt to say, "I have a problem with something that was said the other day, can I talk to you about it?" rather than, "You really hurt me and made me angry."

Blame pins us up against opposite walls with each trying to justify to the other their own position. The removal of blame frees both parties to talk and resolve matters together. I have found relationships healed and enriched when dealt with in this non-threatening way. Ephesians 4:31-32 says, *"Get rid of all bitterness, rage and anger, brawling and slander, along with every kind of malice. Be kind and compassionate to one another, forgiving each other, just as in Christ God forgave you."*

There are many ways that God can help us to resolve issues within relationships. Blaming others is not one of them. On our courses we also give time to pray about blame and here is another prayer if you feel it is an area where you need release:

Lord Jesus

I am sorry for the times when I have harboured bitterness and resentment towards others and blamed them for my hurt and angry feelings. I understand that blaming others is not Your will for me and it hinders my walk with You. I choose now to release *(names of those you have blamed)* from any debt I feel they owe me.

Thank You that when we confess our sins You are *"faithful and just and will forgive us our sins and purify us from all unrighteousness"* (1 John 1:9). I now bring to You all my anger, hurt and frustrations and ask You to be the One to help me get rid of them in a way that allows me to move on in the freedom You have for me.

Thank You, Lord, in advance for all that You will do and for the things You have for me to learn about taking responsibility in this area.

In Your name

Amen

CHAPTER FOURTEEN

Rescue and Humility

Because he loves me, says the Lord,
I will rescue him; I will protect him, for he
acknowledges my name. He will call upon me and
I will answer him; I will be with him in trouble,
I will deliver him and honour him.

(Psalm 91:14-15)

God has a rescue plan for everything in life for those who love Him, even depression.

The earlier verses speak of a range of adversities that may befall a human being: illness, danger, disaster, fear, the devil, things that happen at night and things that happen during the day. They remind us that we are not promised a trouble-free life. Jesus himself says, *"In this world you will have trouble, but take heart, for I have overcome the world"* (John 16:33). The promise is not, therefore, that trouble will be prevented, but that when it comes, He will *act* on our behalf. And five times God says, *"I will"* in verses 14-15, so these are promises to be taken seriously. Adversity is to be seen as an opportunity to experience His power to save and His faithfulness to us in times of trouble. But trouble and adversity also reveal much about our expectations and the attitudes of our hearts.

One of the problems for people who struggle with a depressive illness is that they are not used to receiving help, or expecting to be rescued. The problems very often stem from childhood and having to take on responsibilities too early. If no-one is listening or interested, then children stop asking, and the expectation of help being accessible or available is diminished. It is not that people with depression don't want help, it's just that if it has not been there for a long time, it can take time to sink in that God means what He says. But this too is part of His rescue plan for us. I often used to find myself moved to tears when I witnessed a rescue of any kind, whether it was a pet stuck up a tree or a person in a dangerous or precarious situation. It was something about the nature of the rescuers, their swift response, care and ability. Deep down I think I knew I needed rescuing but did not understand why or how it could happen.

One of the things God began to teach me was that He was a rescuer and that Saviour and rescuer are the same thing. He began to challenge me to look for Him in situations which would usually cause me to panic. Consequently, I found Him in the situation when part of our house was flooded and we had no funds for repairs. I also found Him in the situation when my car had a flat tyre on the motorway whilst I was travelling, with a toddler and a dog, on our moving day from Dartmouth to Farnham. Both times I looked for the rescue rather than at the problem, and each time found there was help and there was a solution. Trusting in His promise to rescue stopped me from giving way to stress and panic and enabled me to see His hand at work. The lessons learned in these external matters of life gave me greater confidence to trust Him to deal with my internally rooted vulnerabilities and fears.

The delight for a Christian, therefore, is not going to be found in living a trouble-free life but in finding God at work in the struggle. But until that is understood, the difficulties of life can become the source of much angst and anger towards God and, in that place, it can be difficult to see Him at work on our behalf.

The book of Ruth has much to teach in this respect, giving insightful examples of different attitudes in severe and adverse circumstances. Both Ruth and Naomi have suffered loss and are destitute. Both perceive God in their situation differently. Naomi says to Ruth, her daughter-in-law, *"It is more bitter for me than for you, because the Lord's hand has gone out against me!"* (Ruth 1:13). But Ruth is not bitter or angry. She simply says to Naomi, *"May the Lord deal with me ever so severely if anything but death separates me from you"* (Ruth 1:17).

There is in this book a wonderful story of God's rescue for both women, beginning when Naomi hears *"... in Moab that the Lord had come to the aid of his people by providing food for them,"* and she *"prepares to return home from there"* (Ruth 1:6). Even though Naomi is embittered by her circumstances and the God who has allowed them, God still works out His rescue plan for her and Ruth. The difficulty for Naomi is that she cannot see it or take comfort from it until she eventually recognises that it is God who has brought Ruth to work in the field of Boaz, a close family member. Then she is able to say, *"He has not stopped showing his kindness to the living and the dead"* (Ruth 2:20).

As Naomi's story shows, our bitter attitudes do not *prevent* God from working in and through our circumstances, but they can prevent us from seeing His hand at work and from receiving His strength when we need it the most. James says, *"Humble yourselves before the Lord so that He may lift you up"* (James 4:10). Throughout the story, it is Ruth who shows humility. Refusing to abandon Naomi, she is willing to be vulnerable in an alien society and go out and find work to provide for them both, saying, *"Let me go to the fields and pick up leftover grain behind anyone in whose eyes I find favour"* (Ruth 2:2).

God's rescue for Naomi and Ruth is complete when Ruth marries Boaz and they have a child called Jesse. But their story also reveals His bigger picture of rescue, since we are told at the end of the book that Jesse will become the father of David, who will later become God's chosen King over Israel and the ancestor of Christ Himself. In the midst of our struggles it is helpful to remember that God not only has a rescue plan for us in our own individual circumstances, but there is also the bigger picture that He is working out too.

There are many today who would say that cultivating a positive attitude is the key to overcoming the adversities of life. It is true that we need a positive attitude. But it will only take us a certain distance and the person suffering with depression will find it very difficult to maintain. A *humble* attitude, however, will enable God to bring His strength to us whilst the difficulties are being worked out. Jesus himself gives us the best example of this:

> *. . . who, being in very nature God, did not consider equality with God something to be grasped, but made himself nothing, taking the very nature of a servant, being made in human likeness. And being found in appearance as a man, he humbled himself and became obedient to death – even death on a cross!*
>
> (Philippians 2:5-7)

In other words:

- Humility takes on the nature of a servant rather than a master
- Humility is thankful for what is and not resentful about what is not
- Humility trusts that God has the answers and waits patiently for them
- Humility does not rage against God when life is difficult
- Humility remembers that salvation is by grace, not by works
- Humility accepts the Word that has been planted
- Humility says, "not my will, Lord, but Yours be done"

Humility also means a greater recognition and acceptance on our part that God has a better rescue plan for us than the one we think we need. Trusting in someone else to rescue us takes time and we need to be prepared for God's rescue to take a different form to the one we thought we needed, as Elijah was to find out when he was faced with threats against him from Jezebel.

CHAPTER FIFTEEN

Rescue: Spiritual and Practical

Elijah was afraid and ran for his life. When he came to Beersheba in Judah, he left his servant there, while he himself went a day's journey into the desert. He came to a broom tree, sat down under it and prayed that he might die. "I have had enough, Lord," he said.

(1 Kings 19:3-4)

Elijah's plan to rescue himself from the threats of Jezebel was to run away. The second thing was to pray that he might die. Some Christians, like Elijah, may have reached the place of giving up and wanting to die, entertaining thoughts of suicide as a way out of their sense of isolation and hopelessness. Elijah brings these thoughts and feelings to God in prayer. We need to help those in such a place to do the same.

God's answer for Elijah, in the first instance, is to give him a place to rest and food to eat. If we are to be God's hands and feet to someone as desperate as Elijah, these verses about how God treats him need to guide us too. It may be that if the person has never been to the doctor to get medical help, this might be a good time to gently talk to them about it. Medication may be the practical help and sustenance they need to stabilise them. Many will be running from current or historical problems they cannot resolve.

One thing that has always struck me is that even when Elijah was running away, God looked after him, giving him food and drink for his journey: *"He looked around, and there by his head was a cake of bread baked over hot coals, and a jar of water"* (1 Kings 19:6). It is important to reassure people of God's faithfulness to them at times like these and that He is the God of the practical as well as the spiritual. When people are exhausted and dispirited, as so many are when they are ill with depression, it is not always about how much they are reading their Bible, praying, or coming to church (important as all these are). As Ruth Hawkey writes, "the wisdom of God shows that there is a time when cake, bread and fish are more necessary than a portion of the Word."[26]

People in this situation will certainly need kindness, understanding and non-judgemental people around them when they feel like this. It took time for God to bring Elijah to a place where He could speak to him about why he was running. Elijah then has the opportunity to pour out everything that has happened.

It has been a privilege to sit with people in prayer and encourage them to do the same. Once the words are spoken, the problems and difficulties articulated, there is very often a shift from hopelessness to a place of peace. Nothing else may happen because nothing else is needed at that point. The unburdening itself can be sufficient to bring a sense of relief and peace. It may also bring a new sense of perspective and clarity about what to do next.

God does not deal with Elijah's problems straightaway. He is simply told to *"Go out and stand on the mountain in the presence of the Lord, for the Lord is about to pass by"* (1 Kings 19:9). There is a further opportunity, in the presence of God, for Elijah to unburden himself again of all that has happened. God then tells Elijah two important things: he must go back the way he came (v15) and things are not as hopeless and desperate as he thinks (v17-18).

God's rescue for those of us who have been running away from problems and the fears associated with them may require us, with His help, *to go back the way [we] came*. It is God Himself who has revealed to me the times when fear has gained a foothold in my life and why. It has been God Himself who has taught me how to work with Him to remove it and allow "His perfect love" to drive it out. Faith, prayer and scripture have been the tools He has taught me to use and exercise in such times, and the blessings have been to experience freedom in areas where I had previously been bound. Elijah has to go back, and God gives him those who will help him to do what is required. In my experience, when God needs to take us back to face difficult and damaging experiences, He will bring others alongside to go with us and support us when we are at our most vulnerable.

And then our perspective too may need readjustment. Things are not always as we think, as Elijah was told. He said, *"I am the only one left and they are trying to kill me too"* (1 Kings 19:14). But God said, *"Yet I reserve seven thousand in Israel – all whose knees have not bowed down to Baal ..."* (1 Kings 19:18). We may draw many conclusions from our situations and circumstances, perceiving them to be as hopeless as Elijah, but God is in control and has plans and purposes that we do not know about. In times of hopelessness, despair and thoughts of giving up on life altogether, it is important to encourage one another to hold onto this truth. The help He has may be both practical and spiritual, but we do need to commit our way to Him if we are to succeed. Our own rescue plans will not work as well as His, as I have also needed to learn.

When I was at my wit's end I sought counselling, believing that it would be a pathway to healing the fear which was crippling me. In some ways it was helpful; I learned about control and I was listened to. However, the encouragement to talk about my fears meant that I left the counselling sessions feeling more fearful week by week. I wanted it to work and kept going, but reluctantly came to the conclusion that I needed to stop. As I did, peace returned, although fear was still present. This, I realised, had been *my* rescue plan for *me*. I was later to find God's rescue for me through two people in our church who understood the crippling nature of fear and how to pray about it. Then things began to really change for the better. I now bring everything to Him in prayer instead of trying to work out the best way forward for myself. Learning about how God rescues has also helped me understand more about trust and obedience.

I knew I struggled with trust and I much preferred rules – I knew where I was with them. But God was calling me into a relationship with Him that was not about rules. I had to make a determined effort to start trusting Him and holding onto His promises. But what if He let me down? I was often assailed with all sorts of doubts and fears but eventually began to absorb the simple truth that God would never let me down, and I began to see how He was working these things out in me as part of my salvation. Obedience too was a 'loaded' word. To me, it meant doing as I was told – or risking punishment. Over time, I have come to see that obedience to God is about blessing and that my mistakes are always redeemable. I know now that His ways are so much better than mine and that His timing in matters of rescue is always perfect.

Many times I have asked Him if He could just heal me all at once. His answer came through this scripture: "*. . . little by little . . . until you have increased enough to take the land*" (Exodus 23:30). I began to understand that it had taken twenty-nine years to become the person I was when He called me, and the changes were not going to happen overnight. I would not have coped if they had.

CHAPTER SIXTEEN

Being listened to and Listening

*The eyes of the Lord are on the righteous and
his ears are attentive to their prayer.*

(1 Peter 3:12)

Whether we feel it or not, God is listening to us when we pray, and He promises action when we cry out to Him. Sometimes, though, depression puts us in such a place of darkness that it is hard to cry out, and when we do, it can be difficult to believe that God hears us, especially when experience has taught us that no-one is really interested. In those times of darkness and apparent silence, I have learned that one-way God will reach people is through the listening of others.

Many with depressive illness will feel that they have never really been listened to. They may have been on the receiving end of much well-meant advice but will not necessarily feel understood or know the benefits of just being listened to. In her book *Listening to Others*, Joyce Huggett writes that when she has asked people how they feel after they have been listened to lovingly and attentively, these are the responses: 'I feel valued', 'I feel comforted', 'I feel as though I can carry on living even though things are tough', 'I feel loved'.[27]

On our courses we include a simple listening exercise so that people can feel the benefit of being listened to and learn the value of being good listeners. In pairs, they take it in turns to tell each other about their struggle with depression. For five minutes one talks and the other listens. The listener cannot write anything down or comment – they only listen. At the end of five minutes the listener tells the speaker what they heard. Then they swap and do the exercise the other way around.

During these short exercises I have observed tears in the unburdening. But I have also observed tears in the *listening*. The deep sense of empathy and understanding that those tears communicated was *this matters, you matter*. Many have needed to carry on after a deep trauma or difficult experience as if it has not mattered or should not matter still. But it does matter and it matters to God. Jesus says that when we meet the needs of the vulnerable, we are acting for Him: *"whatever you did for one of the least of these brothers of mine, you did for me"* (Matthew 25:40).

For most of us listening does not come easily. One of our team brought in these thoughts about listening for us all to consider:

- you come quietly into my world and let me be me
- you hold back your desire to give me advice
- you do not take my problem from me but trust me to deal with it my own way
- you give me enough room to discover for myself what is best
- you allow me the dignity to make my own decisions even though you feel I am wrong.

It is quite a staggering thing to consider that just by listening to someone we may empower them to keep going, or "carry on living even though things are tough". It is something we are keen to continue in our support groups, where there are opportunities for people to share in a safe and supportive environment. We help one another to bring our concerns to God, who knows exactly where we are and how to reach us. He knows too who He can send to help Him answer the needs of our hearts. We can be reassured that even in our darkest of moments He is always there and is always listening. However, it is also important to remember that a relationship with God means a two-way conversation and we need to learn how to listen to Him, as Jesus needed to teach Martha:

> *As Jesus and his disciples were on their way, he came to a village where a woman named Martha opened her home to him. She had a sister called Mary, who sat at the Lord's feet listening to what he said. But Martha was distracted by all the preparations that had to be made.*
>
> (Luke 10:38-40)

Some years ago I was reflecting on these verses and in particular the conversation between Jesus and Martha. In many ways, Martha fits Dr Cantopher's profile of the personality type most likely to become ill with a stress-related depression, since she presents as "reliable, diligent, with a strong conscience and sense of responsibility".[28] When we look at Martha on our courses most people identify with her immediately and feel really sorry for her. Surely it is unfair that she has been left to do all the work by herself, and we can understand only too well her being "distracted by all the preparations", as Luke describes her.

But Jesus' analysis of Martha is somewhat different and goes significantly deeper. He says,

> *Martha, Martha, you are worried and upset about many things, but only one thing is needed. Mary has chosen what is better, and it will not be taken away from her.*
>
> (Luke 10:41-42).

His response, first of all, is to say her name twice. In the distractions of life He may need to do the same for us. We simply cannot hear God when we are cluttered up with distractions and busyness. Secondly, in His statement, "you are worried and upset about many things", Jesus seems to make a *link* between her need to get her jobs all done *with* being "worried and upset about many things". I do not think He is talking about just the tasks of that day. Unresolved worries and troubles tend to accumulate and get heavier over time, and for many the coping mechanism will be to be busy and place an emphasis and priority on the things that need to be done. Many of us, like Martha, will be *"worried and upset about many things"*. These may be things in the present, concerns for the future or unresolved things from our past. As Christians, what we need to be reminded of is that, just as Jesus knew what was going on in Martha, He knows what is going on in us too.

I can easily identify with Martha. When I am worried or upset I preoccupy myself with tasks. I have often wondered whether, if Jesus knocked on my front door when I was in that place of distraction and preoccupation, I would give Him the same priority that Mary was able to do. Would I put the jobs to one side and sit at His feet listening or would I say, "Please come in, I will be with you in a moment, I just need to finish ..."

For some, as is often the case with me, busyness is quite simply a coping mechanism to take our minds off our worries. As a short-term strategy it can be quite helpful until the problem is resolved. But when the problems remain unresolved, this kind of coping mechanism means we are always preoccupied and never really present for the moment. For others, external factors, such as in the workplace, mean the worry of failure, loss of jobs, income, home and more are sufficient to create a cycle where efforts are constantly being redoubled in an attempt to keep their world safe and secure. These worries and troubles about the "many things" we are trying to do inevitably mean God's voice is drowned out and time spent with Him is relegated to a lower level of priority.

Jesus has only one answer for Martha and it is not the one she wants. When Martha asks for Jesus' help she expects Him to send Mary. But He does not. Jesus' answer to Martha is that "only one thing is needed". And it is the same answer for us today. Our worries, troubles and upsets need to be subordinated to our greater need of spending time listening to God. As sorry as we may feel for Martha, Jesus does not send Mary to help her. He does not want her life to be driven by this kind of agenda. Instead, He says, *"Mary has chosen what is better and it will not be taken from her."* He is not saying the tasks are not important or do not need to be done. What He is saying is that it is a question of priorities and we too may need to reverse the order in which we approach our busy lives, even in our service to Him.

Also implicit in His words to Martha is that she is more important to Him than the jobs she wants to do for Him. Sometimes we forget that, and what we want or need to get done begins to dictate how we live. It is very easy in Christian ministry to become burned out. We can, if we are not careful, become strong on service but weak on relationship. There are times when we need to simply *"Be still and know that I am God"* (Psalm 46:10).

In 'learning' the things Jesus wants to teach us, as described in Matthew 11:28-30, this one, I believe, is key. Learning to put Jesus first is vital if we are to overcome in the troubles of life. Jesus' words to Martha are good for everyone to hear, but even more so for those who suffer with a depressive illness. When being busy becomes the coping mechanism when our lives are troubled, we need to reflect on what Jesus says to Martha. That way we have every chance of breaking the cycle of stress which can lead to depression, which will be discussed in the next chapter.

CHAPTER SEVENTEEN

Stress and Depression

In quiet and trust is your strength.

(Isaiah 30:15)

Stress is cited as one of the main factors in the increase of depressive illness. In 2003, Dr Cantopher was writing that "there are several different causes of clinical depression, but by far the commonest ... is stress" and that "up to 1 in 3 consultations in general practice involve patients with the disease."[29] And the problem is not going away. In 2018, an online survey of 4,619 UK residents revealed, "In the past year, 74% of people have felt so stressed they have been overwhelmed or unable to cope."[30]

So what exactly is stress and what causes it? One online dictionary describes stress as "a state of mental or emotional strain or tension resulting from adverse or demanding circumstances."[31] Another dictionary describes stress as a "form of distress" which itself is described as being to do with "great pain or sorrow".[32] There are many known factors that can cause stress in anyone. Bereavement, divorce, moving house, financial worries, pressures at work and at school are but a few. We also live in a fast-paced society with too much to do and too little time to do it. It is difficult for people to escape the negative effects of stress at some level.

Identifying personal stress triggers can be helpful in working out what can be changed and what cannot. As a young mother, I was constantly feeling stressed because there were always jobs that I was not able to get done. One day, I had the presence of mind to sit down and write a list of all the things I did in a day and a list of all the things that still needed doing. Seeing it written down made me realise that my expectations were far too high. There was no way I could do it all, so I stopped worrying about it. Those things not getting done would have to be done another time and not necessarily by me. Also, in our home much stress was caused by not being able to find things. Creating places for things to be put away brought about a greater level of peace within the home.

But not all stress-related problems are solved so easily. The kinds of "mental or emotional strain or tension resulting from adverse or demanding circumstances" are often generated by external circumstances over which we have no control. The stress of trying to achieve what seem to be impossible goals creates an intolerable level of stress, as many find in the workplace and in our education system today. The constant worry of underperformance and underachievement, with no positive encouragement at all, makes those who fit Dr Cantopher's personality type vulnerable to becoming ill with depression, especially when being 'reliable', 'diligent' and 'responsible' do not seem to be valued as highly as profit margins, targets, exam results and league tables.

The reason this type of person becomes ill is because in the face of stress, they will apply a 'try harder' approach to the problem. Dr Cantopher has observed that this type of person "reacts to stress by redoubling of his efforts, pushing himself way beyond the limits for which his body is designed."[33] It is this redoubling of effort that, in the end, makes a person ill.

As Christians, when trying harder is the only strategy we know, it is important that we seek God to help us develop new ones. And the two strategies that the Bible speaks about again and again in times of anguish and difficulty are *trust* and *prayer*. Trust in God is both a strategy and a discipline to be applied so that we can resist the temptation to take matters into our own hands and try to work out solutions for ourselves. Proverbs teaches about trust and what happens when we do; *"Trust in the Lord with all your heart and lean not on your own understanding. In all your ways acknowledge him and he will make your paths straight"* (Proverbs 3:5-7).

Straight paths and strength (Isaiah 30:15) are two consequences of trusting God with our struggles and problems. Leaning on our own understanding and being guided by an overwrought mind is not what is needed. My own strength and resources will inevitably run out and stress is likely to be the outcome, potentially turning into the 'distress' mentioned in the second of our dictionary definitions. But if my heart is already troubled and I am anxious and worried, *prayer* has to be my other new strategy.

In times of difficulty and anguish God is waiting for me to do what the Psalmist does: *"I call on the Lord in my distress and he answers me"* (Psalm 120:1). Subsequently, he writes, *"My help comes from the Lord, the Maker of heaven and earth"* (Psalm 121:1). This, together with Philippians 4:6, reminds us that the God who is in control actually does not want me to be anxious about *anything*. But when I am, I need to be reminded that the Lord is with me and God wants me to talk to Him about it, as Paul testifies:

The Lord is near. Do not be anxious about anything, but in everything, by prayer and petition and with thanksgiving, present your requests to God and the peace of God which transcends all understanding will guard your hearts and minds in Christ Jesus.

(Philippians 4:6)

My heart and my mind need His guardianship, because I know that within me there are the sensitivities and vulnerabilities that Dr Cantopher also identifies in his typical character profile. He writes that this person is "… sensitive, easily hurt by criticism and has a self-esteem which, while it may look robust on the outside, is in fact quite vulnerable and easily dented."[34] I know this is me and I know it is there in many of those I meet on our courses, in our support groups and in times of one-to-one prayers. The diligence is there, the sense of responsibility, the strong conscience and reliability are all there, but underneath are the vulnerabilities and sensitivities that also drive much of how we operate.

I know all the things I have done to cover up how vulnerable I have often felt. I am sensitive to how people respond to me and I have worked hard to avoid criticism by trying to do everything well. My self-esteem is quite easily dented, especially when I am met with disapproval, so I have worked hard to avoid that too. These internal vulnerabilities have made my life a series of highs and lows according to how well I feel I am doing. I realise that my own expectations of myself have driven me to try and live up to impossible standards in an attempt to achieve a level of self-worth and value. Much of my stress, I also realise, has been self-generated in the ways I have tried to overcome my own perceived sense of inadequacy, fear of failure and rejection. Depression itself became a stressor when I could not find the strength to do those things anymore. It made me feel even more exposed and even more vulnerable.

Finding acceptance in Christ has been a major part of my recovery. He is kinder to me than I am to myself, showing me over time that many of the things I have believed about myself are not true. His teaching from Psalm 139 that He always had a plan for me to be here and a purpose for my life has enabled me to shed the belief that my life was somehow a mis-timed mistake on my part. In the past, disapproval from anyone was always an uncomfortable reminder that I still had not reached the required standard for approval and acceptance. My old sense of wrongness about being here at all meant that I easily put myself in the place of failure when I could not meet my own or others' expectations of me. Now if someone disapproves of me I am learning, with the Lord's help, that the problem may be with them and not with me. I feel Him standing with me, defending me and encouraging me. My sensitive filter has become de-sensitised over time but is still a work in progress.

I have also stopped fearing failure in the ways I used to. About twenty years ago I was able to realise an ambition to do a degree in English and Education. I chose a course which did not include exams because I used to fear them so much. As my course progressed, to my horror, exams were re-introduced. But, when it came to doing them, I found I was not scared at all and realised I now preferred this kind of assessment to the many essays I was required to write and submit. Those old internal vulnerabilities had been changed by God over time.

When we have become worriers about life and its problems we need to learn how to step back and listen to the truth of Jesus' words, *"Who of you by worrying can add a single hour to his life?"* (Matthew 6:27). Learning how to take one day at a time can help move our perspective away from the problems of tomorrow and focus our energies on fewer things at a time, as Jesus teaches the crowds, *"... do not worry about tomorrow, for tomorrow will worry about itself. Each day has enough trouble of its own"* (Matthew 6:34). In this, we have to choose whether to be wise or foolish builders. When our lives have come crashing down, it is time to start building *"on the rock"* (Matthew 7:25b).

Sharing our concerns with others and supporting one another through difficult and challenging times is also important. One of our team recently shared that it was the faithful prayers of others that were helping her through a difficult time. God has many ways to help us and teach us to overcome in times of adversity. We need to be in step with Him and we need one another.

Stress left unchecked can sap our energy and our strength. Trust in God renews that strength, and prayer restores our peace. God spoke these words to Paul; *"My grace is sufficient for you, for my power is made perfect in weakness"* (2 Corinthians 12:9). In the end, in Christ, our vulnerabilities will become for us new places of strength as He teaches us more about His grace and power to transform our lives. Staying close to Jesus will also help us to discern when some of our struggle may be to do with the kinds of oppressive spiritual pressures described in Ephesians 6. As we will see, oppression and depression are quite similar in definition and consequence.

CHAPTER EIGHTEEN

Oppression and Depression

The Spirit of the Lord is on me...
to release the oppressed...

(Luke 4:18)

In many ways the Biblical word *oppression* is similar to the secular word *depression*. One dictionary definition describes *oppression* as "A putting on of heavy burdens, hard or cruel usage; and a feeling of heaviness."[35] It sounds like *depression* being very much in line with the burdens and heavy yokings discussed in previous chapters. I believe that this has particular importance and relevance for Christians who struggle with depression because, for some, *oppression* may be a significant component of it.

In reality, *oppression* means that our freedom to be ourselves is being undermined in some way, and not just in the physical sense, as described in Exodus 1:11, where the king *"put slave masters over [the Israelites] to oppress them with forced labour"*.

Emotional oppression can also cause deep depression in some people. Lack of permission to express ourselves through tears and anger, for example, can lead to internalised feelings of pain and anguish. One woman I used to meet and pray with could not cry at all because, as a child, she was told that if she did, she would be given something else to "cry about". Letting go and having a good cry was not an easy option for her. Instead, self-harming had become her way of dealing with deep inner pain. Likewise, suppressed anger can do a great deal of harm. Dr Cantopher writes, "Sometimes it [anger] turns inward and is directed against [the self]", which in turn may lead to self-blame, resulting in a redoubling of effort "to engineer a solution".[36]

In my upbringing, anger was 'bad behaviour' and you were sent to your room for it. As God began a work in me to release my many bottled-up emotions, I was surprised to discover how angry I was. As an adult, I had not considered myself to be an angry person. But I was. And I needed to look to Him for ways of expressing it without hurting myself and others, because at times it felt quite overwhelming. I also began to understand that anger in and of itself is not sin; it is what we do with it that's the problem. Scripture itself acknowledges that there are times when we will be angry *"In your anger do not sin"* (Ephesians 4:26). Bottling it up is not the answer.

But the worst kind of oppression, in my view, is that of the human spirit, where the inner self is held back from functioning and developing as God intended. The crushing or breaking of a person's spirit, discussed in previous chapters, can leave people vulnerable to oppression throughout their lives. I have sat with many Christians who find it difficult to express themselves, hesitant to explain how they feel, for fear of being misunderstood or diminished by the opinions of others. This kind of oppression, characterised by timidity and low self-esteem, together with the assumption that they simply are not good enough or must be doing something wrong, may have been with them for a very long time. The work of setting them free will have begun when they gave their lives to Christ. But for many, like me, it may take some time to release them from their innermost insecurities and negative beliefs about themselves.

On our courses we teach about oppression because it has components of and is similar in definition to depression, and because the Bible teaches about it. It is an area where we can learn how to be overcomers, not in our own strength but with God our Father, Christ our Saviour and the Counsellor the Holy Spirit. But what causes oppression in the first place?

People and circumstances could be held responsible for all kinds of oppression. We can look again at the lives of Elijah and Job as examples; Jezebel was out to get Elijah and murder him, and Job was subjected to one disaster after another. Trauma creates conditions for oppressive thoughts and feelings to begin to manifest themselves in our lives. We may ask ourselves, "Why did God allow" this or that to happen, and in our hearts, begin to blame Him. But that is to misunderstand or not grasp the teachings of the New Testament in this respect. Because behind oppression sits an *oppressor*. And the oppressor needing to be exposed is the devil. Paul writes, *"For our struggle is not against flesh and blood, but against the rulers of this dark world and the spiritual forces of evil in the heavenly realms"* (Ephesians 6:12). Thus, we hear Satan behind Jezebel's murderous threats against Elijah, and we know from scripture that he is the orchestrator of the destruction of Job's life. What is glimpsed in the Old Testament is made perfectly clear in the New. And for many, David's account of suffering through an external enemy's pursuit is one they share in their internal experience:

The enemy pursues me, he crushes me to the ground. He makes me dwell in darkness like those long dead. So my spirit grows faint within me; my heart within me is dismayed.

(Psalm 143:3-4).

The dismay and discouragement that accompanies depressive illness may well have its roots in oppression, past and/or present. The first thing is to *recognise* who our spiritual enemy is. Jesus sums up the devil in these words:

He was a murderer from the beginning, not holding to the truth, for there is no truth in him. When he lies, he speaks his native language, for he is a liar and the father of lies.

(John 8:44).

It is these lies, when believed, that create a gateway for enemy oppression such as doubt, shame, guilt and fear. Many Christians with a depressive illness have a struggle in one or more of these areas. Most of us will not know the lies we have believed and it will be a work of the Holy Spirit to expose them. In my own belief system there were many: *I should not really be here, I am an imposter, people mustn't know this about me, I cannot be loved or accepted if I fail, love is something for other people, not for me,* to name a few. They were sown following times of trauma by *"the ruler of the kingdom of the air"* (Ephesians 2:2), long before I was a Christian. I can look back now and see how much influence such lies had over me.

Jesus says that if we follow Him and hold to His teaching, *". . . you will know the truth and the truth will set you free"* (John 8:32). As He has brought truth into my experience over the years, it has rid me of the shame and fear of not feeling legitimate in my existence. This was a powerful root to the depressive illness I was treated for in later years. This part of it has been dealt with over time through prayer and exercising faith in God's Word and His promises.

Right at the very beginning of His ministry, Jesus said He came, *"to release the oppressed"* (Luke 4:18). But anyone who asks the question "How can a Christian be depressed?" may also ask, "How can a Christian be oppressed?" But being 'born again' is the beginning of freedom, not the end. When lives have been bound up in lies and oppression for a very long time, the work of setting us free may, necessarily, take a while. God did not release the promised land to the Israelites all at once: *"Little by little I will drive [your enemies] out before you, until you have increased enough to take possession of the land"* (Exodus 23:30).

Growth is a process and will need to happen gently and bit by bit for those who are very damaged and broken. Realising that God will often do this work "little by little" is helpful because many will become discouraged when it seems a familiar struggle has come back even after being prayed about. Explaining that it is usually a matter of God wanting to do more in the same area can lift the oppressor's lies sent to discourage us at such times. I have learned to see the enemy's attempts to discourage me in this way as confirmation of my growth and commitment to Christ, not my lack of it. I was not having this kind of struggle when I was not a believer.

The kinds of oppression discussed so far will need wisdom, discernment, love, care and ministry to help a person on the pathway to spiritual health and freedom. We then need to take heed of the teaching of Ephesians 6 to protect ourselves from further oppression in the future. Paul says that as Christians we are to *"put on the full armour of God so that [we] can take [our] stand against the devil's schemes"* (v11). But I cannot do that if I do not know what the schemes are and how they might work against me. C. S. Lewis wrote, "There are two equal and opposite errors into which our race can fall about the devils. One is to disbelieve in their existence. The other is to believe, and to feel an excessive interest in them."[37]

Ephesians 6 was written by Paul to the church in Ephesus, a body of born-again believers, to give them insight and wisdom for the battles they should expect to face. It is worth examining these verses because they hold vital teaching about the kind of struggles we should expect to encounter as believers in Christ, who have crossed over from *"death to life"* (John 5:24). To ignore this teaching or not believe it is, as Lewis writes, an 'error'. When the struggle comes we can quickly become discouraged and, being ill-equipped to deal with the pressures, try to respond with our own ways of trying to work it out. In our weakened state we may even believe the struggle is from God and spend much time in repentance and confession in the belief that the difficult time we are having means we are doing something wrong. But in the invisible realm, the enemy we cannot see can be using our vulnerabilities against us. And while it is working, he will carry on doing it – until we begin to realise what is really happening and start doing what Ephesians 6 says.

In the following chapter, we will examine the pieces of armour we have been given to expose the kinds of 'schemes' we should attribute to our spiritual enemy and, in particular, the ones which may be a component factor in the struggle with depression.

CHAPTER NINETEEN

Armour and Schemes

Finally, be strong in the Lord and in his mighty power. Put on the full armour of God so that you can take your stand against the devil's schemes.

(Ephesians 6:1)

This kind of battle is to be fought in the Lord's strength, not our own, and Paul says we are to put on "the full armour of God" in preparation for *"when the day of evil comes"* (v13). He does not say 'if', he says, 'when', and we may need one another's help when that day comes. It is not always easy to discern the enemy when we are having a difficult struggle. Others may see it before we do, but somebody does need to see it, if we are to be effective in making a 'stand'. Understanding how each piece of armour works will help expose the kinds of 'schemes' we need to be aware of. For Christians with a depressive illness these will often be experienced in disturbed thoughts and feelings such as doubt, fear, false guilt and shame.

Belt of Truth (v14)

Jesus tells us plainly that the devil is a liar: *"When he lies, he speaks his native language, for he is a liar and the father of lies"* (John 8:44). So a key scheme he will use against us is *lies*. It is easy for Christians to believe, for example, the lie that depression has separated them from God. It may *feel* that way, but the Bible holds the truths and promises that we must cling to at times such as this.

> . . . *neither death nor life, neither angels nor demons, neither the present, nor the future, nor any powers, neither height nor depth, nor anything else in all creation, will be able to separate us from the love of God that is in Christ Jesus our Lord.*
>
> (Romans 8:34)

This is a powerful truth to embrace and learn as part of our 'truth armour'. The stronger we become in it, the less likely the enemy will be able to use such lies against us.

Breastplate of righteousness (v14)

Another area of struggle may be in feeling or thinking that we have failed in our Christian walk because we have a depressive illness, leading to feelings of guilt and shame. But our righteousness before God is not to do with perceived failures (or successes) but on the redeeming work of the Cross, as it is written in Romans 3:21: "*. . . righteousness from God comes through faith in Jesus Christ to all who believe.*" But that security of belief can become disturbed in times of vulnerability, and false guilt can begin to creep in. The enemy will often bring back our past mistakes and hold them against us too. But it is a 'scheme' and he is a liar.

Our belt of truth is there to buffer those lies away and the Word of God will defend us. The Psalmists says, "*As far as the east is from the west, so far has he removed our transgressions from us"* (Psalm 103:12). Not only will the Word of God defend us but it is also a weapon of attack, being the *"sword of the Spirit"* (v17). Our frequent use of scripture in such times will discourage the enemy from using these kinds of tactics against us, as will prayer (v18).

Feet fitted with ... readiness (v15)

In the early stages of recovery from a depressive illness, it is important to rest, as we have already discussed in previous chapters. But it is also important to remember that even when we are struggling with depression God can still use us, as we have found through running courses and support groups. The temptation is to believe that we are of no use to anyone and giving up would be the best option. But that would be to believe the enemy's lies and follow him further down the slope of discouragement and despair. Putting one foot in front of the other, regardless of how we feel, is our best defence, as is reminding ourselves of God's faithfulness at all times and in all circumstances. Experiencing His hand on our lives as He steers us through dark and desperate times means we can more easily come alongside others to encourage them to hold on and keep putting one foot in front of the other too.

Shield of faith (v16)

Doubt and fear are two powerful tools the enemy will use to undermine our faith and render us ineffective. His tactics haven't changed since the beginning when he caused Adam and Eve to question God's commands by asking, *"Did God really say ... ?"* (Genesis 3:3). He will try to make us doubt God, causing us to ponder, "Why did God allow?", or "Where is God in this situation?"

Such doubts can afflict even the strongest believer. When John the Baptist was in prison he began to wonder if Jesus really was the One after all and sent his disciples to find out. Jesus replied to them:

> Go back and report to John what you hear and see: The blind receive sight, the lame walk, those who have leprosy are cured, the deaf hear, the dead are raised, and the good news is preached to the poor.
>
> (Matthew 11:5)

I have often reflected on these verses and found them of great help when struggling through times of crippling doubt. I would remind myself of what I knew to be true in my own experience, having *"tasted that the Lord is good"* (1 Peter 2:3), *and* where I could find my experiences supported by scripture. This helped me find the courage to keep going when my thoughts and feelings wanted to drive me in a different direction, because at the root of my problems was the fear of being let down. In the end I had to make a choice to trust Jesus and be determined to make a "stand" against such doubts. For me, it meant being prepared to *"take captive every thought to make it obedient to Christ"* (2 Corinthians 10:5). As I persevered, over time, I found my mind becoming more and more peaceful, my feelings less disturbed and my trust in Christ growing as I determined to do what the scripture said. The verse just quoted is embedded in Paul's reminder to the Corinthian church that the battle is very real and the weapons that we fight with are very real too:

The weapons we fight with are not the weapons of the world. On the contrary, they have divine power to demolish strongholds. We demolish arguments and every pretention that sets itself up against the knowledge of God, and we take captive every thought to make it obedient to Christ.

(2 Corinthians 10:4-5)

The enemy is good at arguments and pretensions, drawing us in by our need to understand, to reason and to rationalise. Processing such thoughts to a satisfactory conclusion to quieten our disturbed hearts and minds is not the answer. Spiritual battles need spiritual solutions, not human ones. Our best defence is to apply the wisdom of scripture, which says, *"Trust in the Lord with all your heart and lean not on your own understanding"* (Proverbs 3:5).

Our shield of faith is also our best defence against fear. Many times this scripture would come to mind, *"Take up your shield of faith with which you can extinguish all the flaming arrows of the evil one"* (Ephesians 6:16). I really was not good at it and often felt overwhelmed by fear. I was very grateful for the prayers of others, which had *"divine power to demolish strongholds"* (2 Corinthians 10:4), and as I began to know greater freedom in this area, I was more able to hold up my shield of faith and sense those flaming arrows falling away before they could touch me.

Some years ago I went to visit a Christian friend who had been diagnosed with cancer and was awaiting her test results. She said that she knew her fears would lie to her. Her faith was very clear and strong and by it she was doing the work of resisting the enemy – by not listening to or processing what her fears wanted her to believe.

Helmet of salvation (v17)

In my early days as a Christian I did not wear this piece of armour well either and often felt feelings of condemnation when I thought I had done something wrong. I have spoken to other Christians who have struggled with feelings like this when depression has made them feel that God is no longer with them.

There are many scriptures that speak of our eternal security in Christ: *"No-one can snatch them out of my hand"* (John 10:28) and *"Having believed, you were marked in him with a seal, the promised Holy Spirit, who is a deposit guaranteeing our inheritance"* (Ephesians 1:13), which are worth knowing off by heart. I have also come to embrace the simple truth of the matter, which is that it is precisely *because I am a believer* that the enemy would seek to use feelings of condemnation against me.

But such is the crushing nature of such feelings that we may need the help and prayers of others to help us recover from this kind of struggle. Perhaps this is also why we are advised to *"Take the helmet of salvation and the sword of the Spirit"* (v17) together in these circumstances. And the Word of God says, *"Therefore, there is now no condemnation for those who are in Christ Jesus"* (Romans 8:1).

On our courses we use a flip chart and divide the page into two columns. We write all the pieces of armour on one side and the enemy's schemes on the other. It helps us to see that there is a very clear line between God and the work of the enemy. One of the devil's schemes will be to try and blur it. We can be confused, for example, between conviction and condemnation, real guilt and false guilt. Jesus makes it clear that *conviction* is from the Holy Spirit: *"When he [the Holy Spirit] comes, he will <u>convict</u> the world* *of sin"* (John 16:8, underline added) and, as we have seen, those who are in Christ are not under condemnation.

Conviction and feelings of *condemnation* are two different things and belong in two different kingdoms. It simply does not make sense, either, for overwhelming fear and love to be coming from the same place because *"perfect love drives out fear"* (1 John 4:18).

Understanding the ways in which we may need to defend ourselves means we can wear our spiritual armour with greater purpose and confidence. Learning to recognise the enemy's schemes also means we can be quicker to take our 'stand' when the need arises. Jesus Himself gives us the best example of how to do this when He encounters Satan in the desert, especially in His use of the words, "it is written" and "it is also written."

CHAPTER TWENTY

Knowing what 'is written' and what 'is also written'

Then Jesus was led by the Spirit into the desert
to be tempted by the devil. After fasting for
forty days and forty nights, he was hungry.
The tempter came to him and said, "If you are the
Son of God, tell these stones to become bread."

(Matthew 4:1-2)

For those who have struggled with a depressive illness, there is much to learn from these verses. The first thing to note is how the enemy targets a potential area of vulnerability. In this case Jesus is hungry, so the temptation is geared towards food. Our vulnerabilities may all be different, but as we have seen, common ones in those with a depressive illness are feelings of guilt, shame, anxiety and failure. These thoughts and feelings are oppressive and can be used against us to create much discouragement and despair.

Jesus uses a scripture about food to resist the temptation presented precisely where He is vulnerable. *"It is written: 'Man does not live on bread alone, but on every word that comes from the mouth of God'"* (Matthew 4:4). We have been given the *"sword of the Spirit, which is the word of*

God" (Ephesians 6:17) to do the same. There are scriptures which speak to feelings of anxiety, failure, guilt and shame, and many Bibles have references at the back pointing to scriptures which encourage in these areas.

Knowing my vulnerabilities towards fear means that one thing I can do is learn some of the scriptures that speak about fear, and there are many. Being able to speak them out helps put fear in its proper context and can help me not to give way to it, as I have found on more than one occasion. But I must position myself in full obedience to Christ if I am to be successful. Taking matters into my own hands will not work and I need the wisdom of the Holy Spirit to keep my eyes open to what is really going on.

The second thing to note is the *strategy* attached to the temptation of Jesus. What the devil really desires is to manipulate Jesus to do what he wants, using His status as a means to accomplish it. *"If you are the Son of God, tell these stones to become bread"* (underline added). Getting the Son of God to do what he wanted would have undermined Jesus' ministry before it had begun. We may experience a similar strategy being used against us if we feel a sense of failure in depression. *"If you were really a Christian ..."* may become a doubt we struggle to deal with. The temptation to question ourselves, our faith and purpose before God may lead us to be manipulated to prove ourselves in ways we do not always realise at the time, such as trying harder and striving in life.

Realising that who we are in Christ is not changed by a depressive illness, and that we have nothing to prove, is to do with embracing and growing in the truth and freedom which God has purposed for us in Christ. Romans 8:33 says, *"Who will bring any charge against those whom God has chosen? It is God who justifies."* I no longer feel stigmatised as a Christian by having a depressive illness because I no longer believe the assumptions and notions which have propped up much of the thinking. Understanding more deeply that I am justified by God means I have no need to prove myself to anyone.

From the example of how Jesus was tempted, we learn too that our spiritual enemy does not give up straight away. What is also revealed is that he will make use of scripture to try and get what he wants.

> Then the devil took him to the highest point of the temple. "If you are the son of God," he said, "throw yourself down. For it is written, 'He will command his angels concerning you, and they will lift you up in your hands so that you will not strike your foot against a stone.'"
>
> (Matthew 4:5-6)

The doubting "if" is now accompanied by scripture making it very persuasive. Many times I have read scriptures which have worried and concerned me that I am failing God in some way. If I were really a Christian, surely I would be doing better, has often been my thinking. Because these thoughts have been generated from my reading of scripture in low times, it has been very difficult not to take it as God's Word for me in my situation. Realising that the enemy can use scripture too has been helpful for me, teaching me that God is not necessarily speaking to me through His word in the context I am being led to understand it. Jesus deals with it with like this: "*It is also written: 'Do not put the Lord your God to the test'*" (Matthew 4:7). Sometimes it is not enough to know just one or two scriptures in our vulnerable areas. We need to know the "it is also written" scriptures to bolster our spiritual armour to silence the enemy and his schemes to trip us up.

So far we have seen that the enemy wants Jesus to *"tell these stones to become bread"* (v3) and to *"throw yourself down"* (v6). What we *say* and *do* often dictates freedom or oppression. If I say to myself over and over again that I cannot go on and that I want to die, without hesitation the enemy will use that to oppress me further. We often speak out what we have been persuaded to believe.

In Christian ministry it is important that such words are brought to the Lord in prayer so that they cannot be used by the enemy in his attempts to manipulate us, to turn our words into actions. But some may have already reached that place, having been persuaded that life holds no further hope or purpose. For them, recommitting their lives to Christ will be an important and necessary step in renouncing the unwitting agreements they have made with the enemy to give in to his temptations and do what he wants.

Finally, the devil reveals his true strategy against Jesus. He shows Him all the kingdoms of the world and their splendour, saying that he will give it all to Jesus if He will bow down and worship him. And that's what he wants. He cannot change our status as Christians, but he will try to render us ineffective if he can. Once again Jesus uses a targeted scripture to counter the enemy's words: *"Away from me, Satan! For it is written: 'Worship the Lord your God and serve him only'"* (v10). This time, the enemy leaves.

Sometimes in ministry the enemy has to be addressed directly. One woman I prayed with many years ago was troubled by recurring thoughts of suicide. As we talked and prayed she said she remembered as a young girl watching from the bedroom window as her adopted mother was being taken to hospital for the very last time. She knew her mother was going to die and wanted to die with her. In prayer we asked God to heal the sorrow she had been carrying from her mother's death. I also felt led to address the enemy as the source of her tormenting suicidal thoughts, commanding him to go in Jesus' name. Afterwards she said she knew she was free and had never imagined that the enemy was at the root of her oppressive thoughts. And that, for many of us, is the problem. We cannot see what is going on, so blame ourselves for being weak in not being able to overcome. As we stay close to Jesus, the Holy Spirit brings wisdom and discernment so that we can minister effectively to one another.

Jesus gives us the perfect example of being *"able to stand, and after you have done everything, to stand"* (Ephesians 6:13). Recognising the "devil's schemes" is the first step to dealing with the problem of oppression. Spiritual battles need spiritual weapons and solutions. Wearing our armour means we can learn how to stand against the enemy and overcome oppression. But we need to be walking closely with Jesus if we are to succeed.

The Bible says Jesus came as the *Son of Man* to seek and save the lost (Luke 19:10). But He also came as the *Son of God* to destroy the devil's work (1 John 3:8). The battle, we must remember, has already been won. Being *"strong in the Lord and in his mighty power"* (Ephesians 6:1) means we can walk in the victory of the Cross where we have previously been *"crushed to the ground"* (Psalm 143:3).

In the following chapter we will consider how God reveals that it is also the 'uncomforted' areas of our lives which can cause us the most difficulty and where we need His restorative touch to bring us back to a position of strength and well-being.

CHAPTER TWENTY-ONE

Comfort

*O afflicted city, lashed by storms and not
comforted, I will build you with stones of turquoise,
your foundations with sapphires. I will make your
battlements of rubies, your gates of sparkling
jewels and all your walls of precious stones . . .
in righteousness you will be established . . .
you will have nothing to fear.*

(Isaiah 54:11-14)

A baby crying out in distress will learn that its mother's comfort restores calm and contentment. But what happens when life has been "lashed by storms" and there has been no comfort, no bringing back to a place of calm and contentment? This picture of broken Jerusalem in exile, needing to be rebuilt, resonates with many lives needing God's healing and restorative touch.

As a new Christian with many struggles going on inside, I read these words one day and knew that God was speaking to me through them, although at the time I did not understand why and what the scripture meant. All I knew was that they spoke to a deep place and I became tearful. My spirit responded in a way that my mind could not comprehend – except that I did understand the first line about not being "comforted". I too had been in "exile" until the age of 29 and there had been afflictions and "storms" in the years that I had not known God. As I read, I was comforted by His deep understanding of where I was in life and the promises of what He was going to do, even though they were yet to come into my experience.

I have come to believe that a root to depressive illness for many lay in the "storms" and the absence of comfort. The problem is not just in the hurting inner self but in the ways we might try to find our own solutions. For Christians struggling with a depressive illness, these verses are helpful to meditate on because they reveal God's heart for those in this situation. And they show the two ways in which we will need His saving grace. The first part is to do with rebuilding what has been broken and the second part is to do with keeping us safe and secure.

The work of rebuilding takes time, and ministering God's comfort to hurting people takes time too. Over the years, through our courses and support groups, we have heard personal stories of loss and trauma where it is almost impossible to perceive how comfort can be ministered. In and of ourselves we can do little. But, as servants of the Living God, we can be used in ways we may not appreciate at the time. For some people, just having a safe place to share what has happened can be the beginning of something new that God is going to do in their lives. Traumas that have never been properly acknowledged by others at the time they happened can be recognised as being what they truly were: devastating, shocking, terrible. Once brought out into the open, bottled up emotions can become freer to express the pain and sorrow of the situation – which in itself can bring relief as God's Spirit begins to work. *Listening*, as we have seen, brings comfort.

Feeling understood, finding encouragement in God's Word, prayers prayed and answered, the quiet reassurances and counsel of the Holy Spirit, the unexpected blessings and somewhere to take our burdens are all available to us as Christians and are means by which God can minister comfort into our lives.

Making our "battlements of rubies" (v12) means we will be less vulnerable to our spiritual enemy, discussed in previous chapters, as we become stronger in Him. Part of God's comfort is also in His discipline and shepherding us away from the ungodly behaviours we may have become entrapped by in times of affliction and "storms" (v11). The Psalmist writes, *"your rod and your staff, they comfort me"* (Psalm 23:4), and for some, repentance will be a necessary part of their healing and restoration.

The outcome of God's rebuilding work in our lives is to establish us in righteousness and cause us to live in peace and security: *"In righteousness you will be established . . . you will have nothing to fear"* (Isaiah 54:14). The picture of God's finished work is one of beauty, resilience, righteousness and peace. All too often we try to sort matters out for ourselves when we could be working with Him towards this instead. In the New Testament, the Apostle Paul writes that when we have experienced God's comfort for ourselves, we are to pass it on to others.

> *Praise be to the God and Father of our Lord Jesus Christ, the Father of compassion and the God of all comfort, who comforts us in all our troubles, so that we can comfort those in any trouble with the comfort we ourselves have received from God.*
>
> (2 Corinthians 1:3-4)

127

For this reason, on our courses we devote a whole session to 'comfort' and the problems associated with it having been absent from our lives. We look at 'safe' things which we traditionally associate with comfort, such as blankets, cuddly toys or a cup of hot chocolate, and we share testimonies of how God has been at work in our lives. We also think about ways we might turn to inappropriate forms of comfort if we are not careful. Then we look at scriptures which speak of God's comfort and His plans for those who may still be struggling with uncomforted areas of trauma and distress. And we pray.

Finding God's comfort in our lives is one of the *treasures* to find as we allow Him to be the one to navigate us through the dark tunnels of depression. In the next chapter we will consider more of the treasures to be found in Christ when we go through such times of difficulty and darkness.

Treasur

*I will give you the treasures of darkness, riches stored
in secret places so that you may know that I am the
Lord, the God of Israel, who calls you by name.*

(Isaiah 45:3)

As I have meditated on these words, I have come to understand their profound significance for a Christian who has lost sight of God in the awful spiritual darkness of a depressive illness. In Colossians 2:3, Paul equates *treasures* with "wisdom" and "knowledge" and *riches* with "complete understanding", all of which are hidden, yet available to us, in Christ.

In the writing of this book, I have tried to lay out the "treasures" and "riches" as I have discovered them over the years. God's wisdom and knowledge about my struggles, what they are, and how and where they started have given me a personal appreciation and understanding of David's words in Psalm 139, *"O Lord, you have searched me and you know me"* (v1).

What I now understand is that God is still God of my situation even when I have lost sight of Him in the dark days of depression. Realising that He can still see me when I cannot see Him is a wonderful reassurance and hope-

all else seems so desperate. That truth, in
f, is a treasure to me. It is a reminder that God's
ess and promises are not dependent on how I feel
an help me in the process of learning to *"live by faith,
t by sight"* (2 Corinthians 5:7).

I believe the promise of *treasures* from God in such
times is one to embrace for ourselves and is in accord
with Romans 8:28, where we read that *"in all things God
works for the good of those who love him"*. God alone knows
how episodes of depression can ultimately be worked into
something good in our experience. The times when He
steps in with a word, a promise or a prompting reminds us
that He knows where we are, how to reach us and what
we need. Like Mary, we can learn to *"treasure up all these
things and ponder them in [our] heart[s]"* (Luke 2:19).

Far from the darkness of depression being a series of
wasted, miserable days, God can use it to show us more
of His grace in ways that will help us to know Him better,
which is the main treasure to be found (v3). One of those
treasures for me was to experience His kindness and patient
promptings to ring the surgery and discuss my symptoms
with my doctor.

I had spent months resisting it, telling myself things
would get better. But I had to accept that things were not
getting better, they were getting worse, and there was the
very real possibility that I would not be able to finish my
degree course. But I feared making the phone call. I would
need to get past the receptionist's probing questions as
to whether or not I was an emergency. I did not feel that I
had a very strong voice for myself to be able to cope with
that. Then I was worried about how to give an account of
myself to the doctor and what *he* might say. But in the end
I made the phone call. To my surprise there had been a

cancellation and I could be seen by my own doctor straight away. I arrived at the surgery rehearsing in my head what to say and how to explain myself, still fearing that I might be dismissed as something of a time-waster. But I went in and found myself able to talk about my symptoms, and my doctor was kindness itself. He said he thought that I had a depressive illness and that some medication would help me back on my feet. I came out of the surgery in tears. Part of it was relief, but the other, more major part was realising that God had been prompting me towards this for some time and I had been resisting. Such experiences also taught me that help from God can come in a number of ways, practical as well as spiritual.

As a consequence of God's leading me to my GP and of taking the prescribed medication I began to recover from depression well enough to complete my degree and I was delighted to come out with a really good result. But that delight was almost robbed away by a chance remark from a friend I had studied with and who had also come out with a good degree. She happened to say she was pleased to have done so well without taking any tablets. I suddenly felt my achievements were not so good after all because clearly I had needed a 'prop'. However, God came to my rescue once again because the thought suddenly came that I too should be pleased because I had managed a good result *despite* having an illness; and I felt upheld. In these examples of how He had guided me and stood by me, I realised I was beginning to know Him better.

On our courses we invite people to consider how helpful it is to put *treasures* and *darkness* side by side and to think about what kinds of "treasures" there are for us to find. Many will think in terms of treasures *in* the darkness and struggle to find anything good there. But the scripture does not say that. It says *of*. Most of these "treasures" will be understood with the benefit of hindsight. We reflect on how God has brought us through previous depressive episodes and what we have learned. We then chart a list of our "treasures", such as recognising His unconditional love and faithfulness, learning to accept help, learning to rest, becoming more self-aware, having more spiritual discernment, friendships, drawing closer to God, the people He has given to help, together with blessings and encouragements to keep going, because it will get better. Every course is different and it is always interesting to hear different things from different people. Opening our minds to the positive aspects of depression and darkness, in the light of God's faithfulness and grace, is a great way to finish our time together. Learning to see our lives through this lens of grace, faithfulness and promise, means our own growing testimonies of how God has worked in our lives will be a wonderful enabling factor for ourselves and others to find the courage to keep going when darkness seems to overtake and envelop our lives. It also helps us to see how we can still be growing as Christians even when in all other respects our lives seem to be 'on hold'.

One area of growth is to develop a much deeper understanding of how *"suffering produces perseverance; perseverance, character; and character, hope"* (Romans 5:5). For Christians with a depressive illness, *hope* is not something that is easily held onto. Knowing that 'hope' will be the outcome of perseverance helps give the struggle some sense of meaning and purpose. The development of character is an important part of that process. The temptation to give up, give way to fear and doubt God in the struggle are all areas that will need to be worked on. I have experience with God to draw on now and am less fearful of life's challenges. I may still not be fully healed from depression, but I am a lot better than I was and I know the treasures He has given me along the way.

In one of our support group meetings recently someone was sharing how they were learning that one of the marks of maturity in Christ is becoming completely dependent on Him. The worldly perspective of maturity is one of self-sufficiency, and many of us will have spent time striving in that direction at some level. If depression teaches us anything, it teaches us that this position is not sustainable and that many are suffering the consequences in their health and well-being as a result. As Christians, our quest is to become mature by *"attaining to the whole measure of the fullness of Christ"* (Ephesians 4:13). If a depressive illness is the catalyst by which some of us get there, opening for us a treasure of grace, we can begin with God's help to turn every negative into a positive for His glory. We can then become for Him those who can be used to shine His light into the darkness for others in the midst of this current epidemic of depression, both in the church and outside.

Depressive Illness and the Christian Course

Depressive Illness and the Christian is a two-day Bible-based course run in Churches around the Surrey and Hampshire areas and more recently reaching out into Essex.

Our format is:

- Teaching
- Small group discussions
- Listening
- Sharing
- Prayer

Over the years we have seen how God can use these times to renew faith and hope in His promise that nothing, not even depression, can separate us from Him.

Information about the course, venues and hosting can be found at: www.depressiveillnessandthechristian.net

You can also find us on Facebook at: www.facebook.com/christianswithdepression.com

Course Feedback

Elaine and team held the Depressive Illness and the Christian course in January this year. It was a gentle time, with a clear Bible-based structure talking about what depressive illness is and why Christians needn't feel guilty. Every person who attended engaged in what was being said whilst seeming relaxed and comfortable. Elaine's understanding of people suffering with anxiety and depression permeated throughout every talk and interaction, with supporting scriptures at every stage pointing the way towards understanding and freedom. The feedback from those who attended was excellent and I know we must do this course again and again to support those people in our churches who are struggling with depression and anxiety; we have to be able to offer them real help. And that is exactly what Elaine delivers. This book will be an excellent resource to anyone struggling in this area.

Susan, Course Host
Finchingfield Church, Essex

Elaine and her team coming to teach us for the weekend about 'Depressive Illness and the Christian' was so helpful, both personally and for others in our church group. She spoke from the Bible and her own experiences in a very gentle and non-judgemental way. For too long depression has been a source of guilt for many Christians. Elaine showed how unhelpful misunderstandings about this illness can be and gave us so much in the way of extra resources as well as time to reflect on our own experiences and ways to support others.

Ruth, Pastoral Team leader
Cornerstone Church, Braintree, Essex

The Depressive Illness and the Christian course was a game changer for me. Not only was the course itself very useful, so much so that I did it twice; the monthly support group following on was really beneficial. I appreciated there being other guys on the course and in the support group. It gave me a chance to open up about non-girlie things. These sessions were relaxed and I felt able to share with everyone. It took me a while to get my head around the 'treasures of darkness', but it has been one of the most important scriptures for me.

Colin
St Saviours Church, Guildford

I was given details of Elaine's course through a church friend. At the time, I was working through a difficult period (these periods have come and gone over the last few years) and I was keen to attend in the hope that I would find ways of dealing with my condition. I am so glad I attended! The course is full of helpful information and provides tools to help understand why we have these thoughts and feelings. It helps recognise areas of our lives that trigger them and where they stem from. Some of Elaine's team talked about their pasts and troubles as well as Elaine sharing her own experiences and how she came to start the course. They gave testimonies, which were encouraging, and I think everyone attending took comfort and encouragement from these over the two days. I would highly recommend Elaine's course and I hope her work continues to help many more to escape the pit we can find ourselves in. Thank you, Elaine, for helping me understand my illness!

Wendy
Linton Free Church, Cambridgeshire

Endnotes

1. who.int/Media Centre, 2017

2. Cantopher, Dr. T. *Depressive Illness: The Curse of the Strong,* 2003, p2 (available at mysurgerywebsite.co.uk)

3. Bedell, G. *Teenage Mental Health Crisis,* 2016

4. Cantopher, Dr. T. *Depressive Illness: The Curse of the Strong,* 2003, p3

5. Ibid

6. Hughes, S. *Seven Steps to Overcoming Depression,* 1982, p1

7. Cantopher, Dr. T. *Depressive Illness: The Curse of the Strong, 2003,* p4

8. Ibid

9. Cantopher, Dr. T. *Depressive Illness: The Curse of the Strong,* 2003, p2

10. Fowke, Dr. R, *Coping with Crises,* 1968, p11

11. Swinney, J. *Through The Dark Woods,* 2006, p38

12. Chambers, O. *My Utmost for His Highest,* 1992, July 5, 'Do not Plan Without God'

13. Cantopher, Dr T. *Depressive Illness: The Curse of the Strong,* 2003, p4

14. Hughes, S. *Seven Steps to Overcoming Depression,* 1982, p13

15. Hawkey, R. *Healing the Human Spirit,* 1996, p17

16. Robinson, Dr K. *Do Schools Kill Creativity?* (2006)

17. Hawkey, R. *Healing the Human Spirit,* 1996, p9

18. Cantopher, Dr T. *Depressive Illness: The Curse of the Strong*, 2003, p3

19. Hawkey, R. *Healing the Human Spirit*, 1996, p62

20. Bedell, G. *Teenage Mental Health Crisis*, 2016

21. Chambers, O. *My Utmost for His Highest*, 1992, 'The Mystery of Believing'/July 18

22. Petersen, E.H. *The Message*/www.biblegateway.com

23. Cantopher, Dr T. *Depressive Illness The Curse of the Strong*, 2003, p2

24. Pytches, M. *A Child No More*, 1991, p53

25. Chambers, O. *My Utmost for His Highest*, 1992, 'The Riches of the Destitute'/November 28

26. Hawkey, R. *Healing the Human Spirit*, (1996), p66

27. Huggett, J. *Listening to Others*, 1988, Preface

28. Cantopher, Dr T. *Depressive Illness: The Curse of the Strong*, 2003, p2

29. Ibid

30. www.mentalhealth.org.uk

31. www.en.oxforddictionaries.com

32. *The Award Compact Dictionary*, 1984, p502

33. Cantopher, Dr T. *Depressive Illness: The Curse of the Strong*, p3

34. Ibid, p2

35. *The Award Compact Dictionary*, 1984, p339

36. Cantopher, Dr T. *Depressive Illness: The Curse of the Strong, 2006*, p19

37. Lewis, C.S. *The Screwtape Letters*, preface, HarperCollins, (2012)

Bibliography

Bedell, G. (2016, February Saturday). Teenage Mental Health Crisis. Retrieved August 17, 2017, from Independent.co.uk: http://www.independent.co.uk

Cantopher, D. T. (2003). Depressive Illness: The Curse of the Strong. Woking, Surrey, United Kingdom: The Priory Hospital.

Cantopher, D. T. (2006). Depressive Illness: The Curse of the Strong. London: Sheldon Press.

Chambers, O. (1992). My Utmost for His Highest. Michigan: Discovery House Publishers.

Fowke, D. R. (1968). Coping With Crises. Eastbourne: Hodder & Stoughton Ltd.

Hawkey, R. (1996). Healing the Human Spirit. Chichester: New Wine Press.

Huggett, J. (1988). Listening to Others. London: Hodder and Stoughton.

Hughes, S. (1982). Seven Steps to Overcoming Depression. London: Marshall Pickering.

Lewis, C. S. The Screwtape Letters. London: HarperCollins, (2012).

Mental Health Foundation. (2018, February). Mental Health

Statistics: Stress. Retrieved November 27, 2018, from https://www.mentalhealth.org.uk: https://www.mentalhealth.org.uk/statistics/mental-health-statistics-stress

Peterson, E. H. (n.d.). www.biblegateway.com. Retrieved May 25, 2018, from www.biblegateway.com: https://www.biblegateway.com/passage/?search=Matthew++11%3A29-30&version=MSG

Pytches, M. (1991). A Child No More. Kent: Hodder and Stoughton.

Robinson, S. K. (2006, February). Do Schools Kill Creativity? Retrieved August 15, 2017, from ted.com: https://www.ted.com/talks/ken_robinson_says_schools_kill_creativity

Swinney, J. (2006). Through the Dark Woods. Oxford: Monarch Books.

The Award Compact Dictionary. (1984). London: Award Publications Limited.

The NIV Study Bible. (1985). London: Hodder & Stoughton.

who.int/Media Centre. (2017, March 30). Retrieved August 15, 2017, from who.int: http://www.who.int

www.clinicaldepression.co.uk. (2007). Retrieved April 2007, from www.clinicaldepression.co.uk

www.en.oxforddictionaries.com. (n.d.). Retrieved April 5, 2018, from https://en.oxforddictionaries.com